# OM For The Mom

By

Vanessa Palmer

**"Happiness is in the palm of your hand – you should take it."**

- Yogi Bhajan

Published by OM PHILOSOPHY and Vanessa Palmer

First Edition 2013

## Medical Disclaimer

This book or the author does not provide medical advice, diagnosis or treatment. The contents of OM FOR THE MOM, such as text, graphics, images, and other material are for informational purposes only. The Content is not intended to be a substitute for professional medical advice, diagnosis, or treatment.

Always seek the advice of your physician or other qualified health provider with any questions you may have regarding a medical condition. Never disregard professional medical advice or delay in seeking it because of something you have read in this book or any form of promotion or advertising for OM FOR THE MOM.

## OM Philosophy

### United States

www.omforthemom.com

email: vanessa@omforthemom.com
facebook.com/omforthemom
twitter.com/vanessaspalmer

TM - OM For The Mom and OM Philosophy are trademarked brands.

ISBN-13: 978-1491076378

# CONTENTS

## SUTRA 1
### *Mind, Body, Spirit*

## SUTRA 3

## After Words

## Contributors Bios

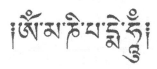

## Author's Note of Thanks

I want to thank a special angel and one of my guides I met last year for sharing these words with me. Thank you, Phillip, for guiding me to unlock my passion and purpose. You said to me, that after all my experience in life my role now was to share and teach. At the time I did not know what that meant, but as I practiced your teachings, your words helped ignite my light for the path that I was meant to walk. So I am now writing this book that has been a dream of mine for years.

If my words, experiences, my trials and tribulations, my Zen formulas, my successes and my failures can teach anybody anything, I have succeeded.

All my friends and family. What can I say, but I am blessed to have so many people in my life, on every corner of the globe that all have shaped my life. There is no life without great people around you to share in all of life's pleasures. You can have the grandest most beautiful home and all the riches in the world, but if there is no one to share it with, you have merely a shell.

I am filled with love from all my blessings and because of this I find so much joy in helping others find enlightenment and through teaching others they also help me grow more and teach me in return. This is the pay it forward rule, the giving and receiving of love. With everything I have been through in life, the one thing I have learnt is this: we are here to love and be loved – everything else is secondary. Those words alone will carry you across the finish line.

**This book is dedicated to all my friends and family that I am blessed to have as part of my life journey all around the world.**

~ My two beautiful children Amira and Malek. My husband Michel, you are all my life, my breath and my sunshine. Thank you for believing in me. You have taught me how to be whole and live a balanced, loving life. I love you all with every ounce of my being.

~ My parents ~ for all that life has given us, I thank you for bringing me into the world and guiding me when you could ~ I hope I have made you proud. I love you both.

~ My brothers and sisters ~ all six of you. ~ Darren, Ben, Ryan, Sarah, Jasmine, Jessica~ I love you all. Jessica, the light in all of us, may your unique and special spirit always shine.

~ My Nana Garton ~ I love you, thank you for always being there for me. You were the only one that could put my hair up and tie my school shoes just the way I liked.

~ Thank you to all the parental figures I had throughout my life. Even though we are not of the same blood, we are connected by love and spirit. You helped raise and love me, when times were difficult in my family ~ you are all my family, I love you all ~ Sue

Jude, Luigi and Lucette -Fiona, Bob and Sandy - Camille, George and Annette.

~ All my life long friends who are great men, fathers, mothers and women who have taken on the world with all its challenges ~ I am so lucky. There are too many of you to list, you know who you are because you are in my life daily – you are like my family. I love you all.

~ A special dedication to Camille, my childhood friend who beat breast cancer with two young children before the age of 40. Kasia, who also beat breast cancer ~ you both are strong graceful women. I love you both and I am proud of your amazing strength.

~ Thank you to Tricia for letting me share your story on falling pregnant with Sophia; I hope your story helps others that are trying to start a family.

~ A blessing to my childhood friend Shevaune who passed away last year at the age of 39 after battling MS for nearly 15 years. You have your angel wings now in heaven. Love and Light.

~ For Angela, a shining star who lives in our hearts forever. You are loved and missed always. May your beautiful spirit soar to heaven.

~ My grandparents, my Aunt Cath and Aunt Mercia that have passed. I still feel you all around me and I know one day we will meet again.

~ I am blessed to have two beautiful God Children. Freddy and Nico, two beautiful Souls ~ I love you both.

~ Karampal Kaur ~ An amazing Kundalini teacher and one of my spiritual guides through this year journey of writing this book. You are a bright, inspiring spirit, thank you for all the breath of fire moments that decompressed me when I was stressed out. Thank you for helping me really go inside of myself and feel at peace while writing this book. Namaste my friend. Sat Nam. Love and light always.

My beautiful sister Sarah, who is the editor of this book. We have a special bond and a passion for living a holistic and spiritual life. My Sat Nam Yoga sidekick and a brilliant writer and Soul, who took all my words and stories and helped me piece them all together. Thank you and I love you with all my heart.

**"Don't walk behind me; I may not lead. Don't walk in front of me; I may not follow. Just walk beside me and be my friend."**

- Albert Camus

*It is time to come out of your cocoon and fly, little Butterfly.*

# { om for the mom }

### noun \ˈōm\

A mantra consisting of the sound \ˈōm\ and used in contemplation of ultimate reality

### noun \mom\

A female parent

### adj \ˈōm for the mom\

A prescription for your Soul and a formula to balance your life. Take the OM pill to become an OM woman \ mom

### noun \ˈōm pill\

A pill of life loaded with OM—ultimate reality. Completely natural. Made up of: the Divine, love, gratitude, happiness, prayer, Yoga, meditation, forgiveness, music, mindful breathing, and too many other ingredients to list.

Taken daily, it causes utter bliss. The Universe has an unlimited supply to prescribe, but is only effective if you live from the inside out.

# *Prelude*

In the 1979 film *Starting Over*, Burt Reynolds' character has a panic attack in Bloomingdale's. His brother calls out, "Does anyone have Valium?" Most of the women in the store open their bags and pull out a bottle of pills.

According to Wikipedia, Valium (known generically as diazepam) has been one of the most prescribed medications since it was first introduced in 1963. The drug of choice became such a hit that in 1966 the Rolling Stones wrote a song called "Mother's Little Helper," a reference to the little pill's new nickname.

As the feminist movement took over in the 60s and 70s women became more independent and powerful, and they were ready to break out of the four walls of the 1950s. The dramatic shift of women's roles in society forever changed how women viewed their life. The dreams and desires they were harbouring inside could now possibly take flight. It was a new era, and there was nothing that was going to hold these wonder women back from being and doing it all.

There was a little issue, though, with this newfound freedom— time. How could everything be done? Go to work, look after the kids, do homework, take them to school, wash the diapers, make breakfast, lunch, dinner, grocery shop, pay bills, go to the beauty salon, exercise, answer the phone, do laundry, clean the house, tuck the kids in bed—and then be the perfect wife waiting in bed, wearing a little negligee for your husband.

The routine may sound familiar to many, but remember that this was all before the modern age of conveniences such as the internet, mobile phones, text messaging, Peapod, disposable diapers, online bill pay, take out, and dry cleaners. Mother needed some help to get her through the day to stay as calm as possible—a little blue pill would be just the thing to calm the nerves and get her through her busy life. What a little miracle.

Today, while there are a lot of little pills still readily available (and taken for people that really need them), there is also a powerful cultural shift towards embracing holistic well-being as the means to a more calm, centered, and vibrant life. Taking great care of Mind, Body, and Spirit in equal measure is the greatest gift you can ever give yourself.

In the Age of Information we have access to a full spectrum of spiritual and secular traditions from all around the world, and we have the luxury of drawing on knowledge from all of them. We get to see common threads among traditions from opposite sides of the planet and separated by thousands of years, and we can see how these threads weave together to form the fabric of human wisdom.

The key to reconnecting with ourselves is embracing this collective wisdom and listening to the truths that resonate with your spirit. Once you make this ultimate connection to the self, you become calm, centered, energized, and prepared to face anything life throws your way.

So what is this wisdom? And how do you embrace it?

It is all around you. All you must do is open your heart and mind. If you walk into the Self Help section of any bookstore, you will find shelves upon shelves of information on living a happy and fulfilled life. An even wider array of information is available on the Internet.

To develop your own personal formula for a blissful, holistic life, you should be open to trying some new things. When you find something that resonates with you and makes you feel more alive, then stick with it.

I have been developing, practicing, and refining my own holistic and spiritual formula now for over twelve years, and every day it is a conscious effort and a learning experience. I have read at least 100 self help books. Books on Buddhism, life on the other side—you name it; it's in my collection.

I have experimented using different tools and techniques and tried many forms of exercise, meditation, and Yoga to discover what works for me. I even started a spiritual and holistic wellness spa. I studied Reiki to learn the simple lesson that we are all pure energy. I have even journeyed throughout Asia and chanted in temples, observed the daily rituals of Buddhist monks, and immersed myself in other cultures, where it seems effortless to connect to the simple pleasures and moments we so forget in the Western world. I became a "spirit sponge." There was nothing that I did not delve into to learn more, and beyond that, learn how to feel more.

In short, I have put in a lot of work, and it has bought me absolute happiness. There is no other way do to it. You must do the work. What works for my life may not work for yours, but you will never know what is right for you until you start walking the path. There is a difference in knowing the path and walking the path. Once you start applying the formula to your everyday life, you must continue to do the work to stay on your path.

In his book Outliers, Malcolm Gladwell posits that if you work at anything consistently for over ten years (10,000 hours) you can claim to be an expert or master in almost anything. A master of life, though? No, I make no claims at that. Can life be really mastered? I don't believe so. Nobody can claim to have mastered life because it is an ever-changing, ever-evolving lesson. Although I cannot claim to be a master of life, I am nonetheless at a point in my life where the calling to pass on what I have learned thus far is strong. This passion is what drove me to write this book.

I am at a point in my life where giving something back to the world that has given me so many blessings is my calling. I want to tap into my ability to guide and influence others in a positive way and guide them toward fulfilling their dreams and desires in life. I have come to find the simplest and most precious gift we can give others is to act as a positive example of conscious living. I want to help others access their guidance systems that enable them to make the soundest decisions and create a life full of happiness and abundance.

Before you start doing the work, you must accept that there is no perfect life that you can create. There is no human being on this Earth that has been spared a life of heartache, loss, troubled water, and pain. Challenges are essential for personal growth and necessary for the Soul to flourish and evolve. Without bad we cannot know what good is. What would be the comparison? Without strife we would not understand the true meaning of gratitude or recognize our continual blessings for what they are.

Gratitude is a word you will hear a lot throughout this book. At least twice a day I close my eyes and thank God for my blessings. Even if my blessings for that day were as simple as being free from back pain or having food in the fridge. Remembering that the simple, everyday things we so often take for granted are the same things that someone else prays for in earnest.

If you are looking for a quick fix or a magic pill to make your life blissful, this book probably isn't for you. Then again, nothing that happens in life is an accident, a coincidence, or a mistake; so if you are reading this book right now, then something inside you knows what you really need to do.

One thing I can promise you is that once you practice conscious living, do the work, and apply it to your life, it will become part of you. You will do it without even thinking about it most of the time. This is called detaching from the ego, aligning with your authentic self and connecting to the source. Your life will flow. Things will fall into place. You will see the signs and confirmations that you're on the right path, and doors will open for you. The right people will appear and stay in your life, and the ones you don't need will magically step out of your energy source.

You will feel at peace, and you will be happy—so happy it will become infectious. You will be doing what you love in life. You will attract everything you need, and you will be happy with what you need, not with what you want. You will be grateful for all blessings large and small, and everything will excite you.

Sounds like you're on some kind of happy drug doesn't it? It's called the drug of life, and it's a cliché for a reason. Fully abundant, endless refills, and can cause utter bliss.

This journey I am about to take you on is inspired by my story, but I want it to become your story. It tells you a bit about how I overcame life's obstacles to find my own formula for bliss, and I hope it inspires you to do the same.

Thank you for letting me share my story and my spiritual formula with you. You can be everything you want to be, finally find out what you're here to do, and really make the most out of this crazy, beautiful ride that we call life.

*Every single person is the artist and author of their own destiny. This journey is yours. Take it; give yourself wings and set flight.*

## *How To Use This Book*

Regardless of your childhood upbringing, your religion, culture, or beliefs, we are all from the One source. Whatever your philosophy or creed, picking up this book and giving it your energy is the first step on your new path to discovery. Half the battle is letting go of the shell you have built up around you and just being open to the possibility of the magic this Universe has to offer.

When you discover your true authentic self, and when that person shows up for you every day, you have then found Enlightenment.

You may be a non-believer, Christian, Jewish, Muslim, Hindi, or Buddhist. None of that matters because there is no box in the spiritual realm—you are a part of a vast, expansive Universe that has no boundaries.

You may be spiritually evolved and just want to find new ways to continue doing the work. You may want to add more balance to your life or leap into a new career or business that passionately excites you. Utilizing the tools in this book will help you be a better woman or mother.

If you are new to this whole self-exploration thing, I say jump off the cliff and soar. If you do the work you will find peace, love, happiness, and abundance. Most of all, you will find yourself. I only hope this book will help you crack the surface, to light a spark and turn any darkness into a very bright light.

Throughout this book I will share a lot of my ingredients that go into my OM Formula for life. If it resonates with your energy, journal it and put it in your formula.

Whenever you see the OM ॐ symbol throughout this book, this is meant for you to pause, breathe, and think about what has been said. You will also see the words **Inhale ~ Exhale**. When you see this, close your eyes, think about what was said, and practice mindful breathing, in through your nose and out through your nose. This will let the thought resonate with your energy and lock it in. **Inhale ~ Exhale** wherever you need to in this book.

This is how you get through life, and using the tool of mindful breathing is extremely important.

*Burn your favorite incense, candle or oils while reading. Make yourself a hot cup of tea and find a sanctuary your favorite resting space to read in. Most important, bring good energy to your space when reading this book. It will help the book resonate with your energy in a more positive way. You are responsible for the energy you create. You are responsible for the energy you bring into your space.*

*Take notes, write in your own journal, start your own story and formula for creating your blissful life. Do the work and I promise you will feel as happy and blessed as I do.*

# Sūtra

I have replaced the word "chapter" with "Sutra" in the three main sections of this book.

"A sutra is an aphorism (line, rule, formula) or a collection of such aphorisms in the form of a manual or, more broadly, a text in Hinduism or Buddhism. Literally it means a thread or line that holds things together".

-Wikipedia

## *Om Mani Padme Hum*

*Mani means, "jewel" or "bead" and Padme means "the lotus flower", the Buddhist Sacred Flower.*

I have also included a glossary of terms, a selection of my favourite quotes, music, apps, meditations, tools and resources at the end of this book.

*Namaste my friends. Enjoy your journey.*

# *Sutra I*

## *Mind, Body, Spirit*

Connect and find your beautiful inner being—your true self.

Spirit is the part of you drawn to love, hope, and gratitude. We all walk a journey that constantly unfolds before our eyes.
So open your eyes but look with your heart. Quiet your mind to listen to the voice. You are a spiritual being, living a human existence.
*It's time to connect.*

*What is Spirit? Well, it's the light in you.*

The first section of this book is called Mind, Body, Spirit. I wrote this section first because I fundamentally believe that before you get married, enter into a relationship, start a family, start a business, go back to work, or try to change your life and get on the path you dream of, you must first become intimately acquainted with your true self. Only then can you make the right choices for your life.

You will have to rip yourself apart, get uncomfortable, and look at your real self without the mist of the ego. You are going to have to do the work. You will have to face the dark parts of yourself that you don't like, accept them, and take ownership of them in order to let them go.

Sometimes you will get stuck, disconnected, and fall apart. That's ok. I still have these days, and I have been practicing spiritual work, Yoga, and meditation for over 12 years. Get used to this. It's called "being human." We are here to learn the lessons and do the work. If we were perfect we would be on the other side, rather than here on Earth for the specific purpose of evolving our Soul. In this life we will all experience both success and failure; one does not live without the other.

I have included in this section many tips, products, and techniques I use in my life to enhance my spirit. They are all part of my Spiritual OM formula. You will figure out what you are drawn to and what is right for you; first you just have to do the work and try it.

*Create and live in a world more holistic and less materialistic.*

I don't talk a lot about manifesting money in this book. I will explain why. I have been around a lot of money in my life; my father was a self-made millionaire by the age of 30. I lived a life of financial abundance growing up, and I am eternally grateful for everything my family provided for me. World travel, experiences, education, opportunity, and too many other things to list. But I have also seen the heartache and troubles money can bring. I have seen what it turns people into, the bad people that hover around you, and all the pain it can attract.

Money can bring you wonderful things in life. You can do a lot of great things with it, and it does make life easier in many ways. But trust me - know who you are first. Get rid of operating out of your ego, do the work on yourself, and operate from your heart. Do what you love and then money will be one of the rewards for your service and efforts. When you acquire it, be humble. Give to others in need and help wherever you can. Money does not make you a better person. I can't emphasize this enough. Do what you love and the rest will follow. Create your formula and do the work, and it will all flow.

**"Possession of material riches without inner peace is like dying of thirst while bathing in a lake."**

- Paramahansa Yogananda

When you start working on your mind, body, and spirit in unison, you will soon start to magically create your own holistic and spiritual formula for your life - your very own unique blend and potion that works just for you. You will tweak it, change the ingredients now and then, and sometimes change the formula to suit your life at any given time - there are no rules. You will discover new things in life and the Universe will magically start sending you things you need. Little miracles and new ingredients for your formula will just start showing up.

I recommend keeping a journal with you as you read this book and make as many notes as you need to. Eventually, once you start practicing and incorporating the formula into your life, things will start flowing. Ideas will come to you when you're in bed, dreaming, meditating, out walking, in the park, engaging in Yoga or exercise, driving in the car, or relaxing in the shower or bath.

Once you figure out the spiritual side and lay that foundation for yourself you will make the right choices and follow your blueprint and purpose in this life. Remember: your thoughts become things. You have the gift of choice and can manifest everything you need into your life to walk a very happy, simple, and successful journey here on this Earth.

## The Journey Begins

We are all on a journey of spiritual growth that starts from birth and even well before then. Even when we are spiritually stagnant and not exactly evolving, we are still on our paths. Sometimes we rest, sometimes we divert, but there always comes a time to move on and move forward. Everything we do is all a part of the journey toward self-realization and enlightenment. When we first begin to realize that we are on a journey, that we always have been, that moment is a whole new beginning.

Where did my journey begin? Well, I started reading. I started to read every book I could get my hands on that delved into spirituality and life after death. I started to study and follow the teachings of many inspirational and enlightened Souls, such as the Dalai Lama and Deepak Chopra. I read just as many books on motivation and self help. I have a bookcase in my house filled with these kinds of books—so many that I could open a spiritual library.

There are a lot of people out there doing the work, so many spiritual entrepreneurs, healers and story tellers, and that is what the world needs now more then ever to evolve. Each book I have read has given me a piece of a giant puzzle that has been embedded in my Soul. I live and breathe what I have learnt thus far, and with that knowledge and practice I have arrived at my destiny to write this book.

I opened my own Spiritual Spa for women when I was 30 and learned everything from reiki, to energy work and unique couples connection therapies. We offered Yoga and meditation, and every service was developed based on healing and uplifting the spirit- it was like a spiritual school.

I love creating experiences, guiding and helping someone feel good about themselves while helping create subtle and sometimes radical shifts to change people's lives for the better. I became addicted to this area of work and decided ten years ago that whatever I did there on out, my life had to be driven by the spirit. There could be no other way.

It is the simple things for me that help get me through my life as a busy mother of two and a wife, running my own business and looking after myself. It is not always perfect, but I accept this as life. I try and get it right 80% of the time, and I think that is a pretty realistic goal to live by. There are days I am down, sad and disconnected, but I no longer allow myself to stay there for too long. I work at getting out of the rut and connecting myself back to the source.

I work every day at living a conscious life with purpose. I do this work because I know this is the only way to happiness. It makes me a better mother, wife and friend. It helps me see my dreams and visions clearly to guide me, keep me on my path, and to turn my dreams into reality.

*The Divine*
*The One*
*The Universe*
*The Creator*
*God*

ༀ་མ་ཎི་པ་དྨེ་ཧཱུྃ༔

"I looked in the temples, churches and mosques, but I found the Divine within my heart."

- Rumi

"We can reject everything else: religion, ideology, all received wisdom. But we cannot escape the necessity of love and compassion. This, then, is my true religion, my simple faith. In this sense, there is no need for temple or church, for mosque or synagogue, no need for complicated philosophy, doctrine or dogma."

- Dalai Lama XIV

Spiritual enlightenment is not governed by any religion. Enlightenment is a state of being you find within yourself. It is a place inside that resonates with pure love.

I spent most of my youth and adolescence being raised as a Catholic. I was baptised a Catholic, I made my first communion and my confirmation, I went to confession, and I spent most Sundays in church. I attended a Catholic grade school and a private girls' convent in my high school years. Although I wanted to believe in a higher power, somehow the Church's messages never really resonated with me. Maybe I wasn't ready to listen.

During my late adolescence and early twenties I was entirely disconnected from anything remotely spiritual. I believed in God, but I did not know how to connect or to feel the divine truly inside of me.

I know that I'm not alone in this experience because I have shared countless conversations with others on the subject. I believe this is a very real problem in society today, at least in the USA and Australia; I can't speak for other cultures with which I am not so intimately familiar. I have seen so many people yearning to believe, wanting to find answers but just not knowing where to look.

I believe that all religions are beautiful, and I have become well enough acquainted with many of the major religions to know one thing for sure—we all pray, practice compassion, and connect to a higher power. The same higher power.

In Judaism, the most ancient name for God is Yahweh (YHWH), which roughly translates as, "I am who I am." In Islam, Allah is the Arabic word for God. Muslims don't pray to another God—it's the same one.

Practicing Muslims pray five times a day. You place a mat on the ground, get down on your knees, and put your forehead to the Earth with hands cupped to the heavens to thank God for all His blessings. When I started practicing Yoga, I realized that its flow and movement were so similar to the act of prayer, only labelled differently. Many other religions and faiths share similar rituals—getting on hands and/or knees, looking up or out to the heavens, and praying to that simple, loving connection.

Finding spirituality just means connecting to God, the Divine. How you get there, the method you practice, that's your personal technique. It is not the only way; it's just your way. What is right for some does not resonate with others, and people just have to learn to accept that. If the world operated like this, if people would only let one another live their own lives and follow their own beliefs, our world would be a much more peaceful place.

Like me, there are a lot of people in my generation and the younger generation who have found God in other ways aside from in temples, mosques, synagogues, or churches. God—the Divine— is everywhere. I can connect to him in silence in my home, on my bed, out in nature, on the beach, and in Yoga and meditation rooms. I know that I need only to close my eyes, breathe, feel the Divine inside, and start to pray. I just have to be in silence to really hear His voice. The practice of meditation has taught me to quiet my mind and slows everything down so I can listen to that silent inner voice, the whispers in my heart.

However you refer to Him (or Her)—The Divine, Allah, Baha, Jehovah, Yahweh, The Creator, The Almighty, The Universe, The Infinite, Our Father, The Spirit, or God—does not matter. As long as you know that you are connected to a greater being and infinite energy that guides you to live your life through pure love, that is all He expects of you. Your religion is your relationship with God.

You don't have to throw away your religious beliefs to embrace spirituality; you just have to me more open minded, believing that God cannot and does not operate in a box. Unfortunately, there are often many dogmatic issues and intolerances that are packaged with religions, and these regimented notions can put God in a box, making people fearful to think outside of those boundaries. Spirituality, however, is the experience of feeling God's—the Universe's—unconditional love, with no boundaries. This is a love that fills you to the point of overflowing, a connection so powerful that you want only to love and give to others, without any fear.

**I hear God in the still, small voice inside of me. To hear His voice I have to quiet my mind. This is where meditation becomes so powerful; it disciplines you to stop, pause, and use your power of the Divine within you, without depending on a doctorate of dogma. Even the Bible speaks of the divinity within us.**

*As Jesus said, "The Kingdom is in you."*

*Everything is Energy*

*[Including Us]*

**"We are spiritual beings having a Human experience."**

- Pierre Teilhard de Chardin

When I began reading and studying books on spirituality and the afterlife, I immediately noticed a prevalent theme—the simple but powerful message that everything is pure energy, including us. We are all giant, electrically charged balls of energy.

Whenever I explain this to people who are first learning about spirituality, they tend to look perplexed and confused. And why shouldn't they be? As human beings we appear as giant masses of matter—physical bodies.

One of my many spiritual guides told me that in my teachings I should try to explain this to people in the simplest form possible so it would be easy to understand. The very basis of your spiritual foundation rests upon understanding this principle. Once you truly understand this, everything else I talk about in this book will make more sense, especially the principle of attracting and manifesting everything into your life – The Law of Attraction.

Although the physical world around us appears solid, everything in the Universe, including human beings, is made up of 99.99% empty space. This is a scientific fact, as taught in a high school physics class. We know this because atoms—which form molecules, which form cells, which form tissue, which form organs and systems, which form our bodies—are 99.99% empty space.

Take a moment to stop and consider this fact. Even if this is something that you already know, take a moment to think about it, to picture it. Every time I pause to reflect on this truth, I am filled with a sense of awe and wonderment.

So how is it that the physical world appears so solid? The answer is Energy.

Figure 1 depicts an atom; with a cloud of electrons orbiting its nucleus in a way reminiscent of (but not exactly like) the way planets orbit our sun. Actually, the electrons' orbit is in many ways like a cloud of gnats circling in space. The movement appears chaotic and random up close, but viewed from a distance the cloud appears contained, the individual components moving together through space as one unit.

**Figure 1: "An Atom"**

Electrons move so rapidly as they circle the nucleus that the empty space seems to disappear, and the atom seems less like a chaotic cloud and more like a solid unit. But the empty space is still there. The glue that holds this whole configuration together is energy—an electrical charge that keeps the electrons moving, pulls them toward the center of the atom, and keeps the whole thing from falling apart.

These tiny, wonderful atoms that are 99.99% empty space and buzzing with energy are the building blocks of everything in the physical world, including us.

On a larger scale, this energy manifests itself as vibrations. Everything, including yourself, your thoughts, and anything else you may or may not want to experience, is pure energy vibrating at different frequencies.

The first time I ever experienced and understood this principle was when I was receiving a Reiki session by an energy therapist at my spa. Kathleen hovered her hand over my crown chakra (at the top of my head) and started moving it around in circles in the air. The crown chakra is the seventh chakra and is the foundation for our spiritual body, linking us to the highest universal and divine guidance.

At first I felt nothing, but after about five minutes the soft Zen music that was playing in the room began to sound very different. The music morphed into an eloquent whirl of space and sound, thrumming with vibration and singing like a crystal glass does when you trace a finger around its rim.

When I asked her why the music was doing that she said, "Look up and look at my hand." I tilted my head back and saw the circular motion her hand was making above me. I realized with awe that the music was dancing and churning to the rhythm of her movements, as if she were conducting some divine orchestra from another realm.

It was beautiful. For the first time I understood that we are all pure energy, that the auras radiating from our bodies are nothing but giant fields of electro-magnetic energy.

## Light Energy Takes You Higher

**Higher Frequency E-Motions**: Love, Happiness, Gratitude, Giving, Compassion, Truth and Peace

## Heavy, Dense Energy Takes You Lower

**Lower Frequency E-Motions**: Greed, Anger, Fear, Hate, Jealousy

I have read in many books that when we cross over to Heaven we are vibrating at a higher frequency. Happy, good energy floats higher to the heavens and negative, heavy energy sits lower in a zone like hell. When you think about it, it really is no different than how we connect with people here on Earth. As the old saying goes, "Birds of a feather flock together."

You will always find like-minded people with similar energy connected or cohabiting together. Think about the difference between a Tibetan Ashram in the Himalayas with peaceful monks, as opposed to a ghetto full of violent gangs. Your energy grows where your energy flows.

# *Your Soul*

**"My Soul is from elsewhere, I'm sure of that,
and I intend to end up there."**

- Rumi

What is a Soul? Well, to answer that simply, to me a Soul is who you are, and a body is what you have. Understanding and applying this simple message to your life is certainly a challenge in the physical world you live in. You are incarnated in a body when you are born to this Earth, but at your core you are a spiritual being and a Soul. It is through your body here on Earth, in this physical world, that you can experience life and all it has to offer. Through this experience you teach your Soul in order to learn, grow, and evolve.

Your Soul is the essence of who you truly are without the body and ego that are attached to you in this physical world. Although you need both the ego and the physical body to function in this world, the path to spiritual enlightenment here on Earth begins with doing the work that gives birth to your true, authentic self and allows the Soul to glow in all its glory. The Soul can also be referred to as your Divine, your Spirit, or your Essence, and this is the part of you that, when ignited, takes control to lead you to your life's true destiny. When you lead with your Soul you will never be lost.

The body is merely a vessel for your Soul, and the Ego can be both the Soul's worst enemy and its greatest teacher. Our Ego wishes for us to stand out and be someone special. It craves recognition and attention. The Ego has a voracious appetite and is never satisfied with what it gets because the nature of the Ego is never to be satisfied. Its recognition comes at the expense of others, and it constantly seeks to be better than or even worse than others at any cost. It does anything and everything to stand out from the crowd of other egos on this Earth.

Your Soul, on the other hand, always feels grateful and complete, doesn't need recognition or glory, and revels in the simple pleasures of life. When the Ego takes charge it wants fame, money, power, and glory—and the need to be right, always. When the Soul takes charge, it wants love, peace, gratitude, compassion, and acceptance of 'what is' to take charge of its life.

Fame, money, power, and knowing what's right should only be the result and the reward for you doing your Soul's work. That's why people who seek money and fame for their own sakes find when they get them they are still unhappy. All they have then are things to feed the Ego, not the Soul, which is the true source of all contentment.

Understanding the two simple principles that you are pure energy and that you are a Soul are "Spiritual 101" lessons, but they are extremely important to cement into the foundation you'll need in order to do the work that will set you on your life's path.

Master the simple principle that everything you do should be driven by and for your Soul, and then you can start to move mountains.

Feed, fuel, and nourish the Soul, and you will never walk another day on this Earth starving for happiness.

*Manifest and Attract Your Life*

**"All that we are is the result of what we have thought."**

- Buddha

*The first and foremost rule to attract all the things you want in life is that you must first believe it can happen and be ready to do the work to make your dream a reality.*

*To see the divine's messages on Earth, we must open our eyes, heart and Soul to see them. Life whispers to us, but you have to listen closely.*

In the chapter, "Everything is Energy (Including Us)," I touched upon the principle that our thoughts and emotions, in addition to our physical and spiritual bodies, are made of pure energy. This chapter explores the implications of our energetic thoughts.

When the documentary "The Secret" first came out, I was one of the first people to get my hands on a copy. The Secret was not a new phenomenon, but simply a new visual story on an age-old law of the Universe, the Law of Attraction. (Note: if you have not yet seen this life-changing documentary, what are you waiting for?)

The biggest misconception about the Law of Attraction practice is how you actually go about getting the things you want out of life. The simplest rule is that to get what you want, you must focus on what you want—don't think about what you don't want or what you fear because you will attract that instead.

Focusing your attention on what you want will not get you anywhere, though, if you do not also take action to bring your dreams to you. You can't just sit back, dream, and think, "I want a million dollars," without ever getting off the couch to go make it. You can't expect to meet the love of your life but never make the effort to go out and meet people and try to connect with others.

I have to laugh whenever I hear people say, "The Secret doesn't work." I ask them, "What effort have you actually put into creating and manifesting your dream? Did you pray and dedicate every ounce of passion, love, and commitment to making your dream come true? Did you do the work?" Of course, the most common answer is, "Well, no. When you put it that way, no, I didn't do that."

We live in a society today that expects immediate results. When something breaks or cracks we don't repair it, we throw it away. When something becomes challenging, we give up all too quickly. If you give up on something because it is taking too long, then maybe you just don't want it badly enough to make it happen. Maybe you aren't ready, or maybe what you think you want is not actually part of your universal plan. Maybe it's not mapped in to the blueprint of your life. Or maybe you don't believe that you can make your dreams come true. Maybe you are afraid to fail. Maybe you are afraid to succeed.

When you operate out of love and listen to the whispers of your heart, signs start to appear, and your inner voice starts speaking louder. What you want out of life becomes clear, and fear falls by the wayside.

When you allow your true self to be your guide, you—not your ego, you—will be led to the gate of the palace of your wildest dreams. You will hold the key to open that gate to the world you want to create. You will do this effortlessly, and it won't feel like work. You will feel you need this in your life just as much as you need to breathe to stay alive. If you don't have that feeling, step aside and delve further into your inner wellspring; clear out more dirt and rocks to find the water you need to sustain your Soul.

When you attract what you love in life, that inner presence radiates as friendliness and kindness, and those qualities will naturally draw the right people, jobs, situations, and experiences closer to you. Don't worry about the money. That will follow as a result of what you are doing.

If all you think about is money, you can go out get a job that makes you lots of money, but you will most likely be stressed and hate what you do. When you operate this way you are not connecting to the space that was intended for you, carved out by the Divine when he laid out the blueprint of your life.

**"A slack hand causes poverty, but the hand of the diligent makes rich."**

- Proverbs 10:4

The Law of Attraction is not just about attracting bliss. You will attract everything in your life that you need in order to evolve your Soul and enlighten your spirit. There will be challenges, trials and heartaches that you think you do not deserve, but these appear in our lives because they are necessary for the growth of the human spirit.

One thing I know for sure is that if you are walking your path, connected to the Divine, and operating out of love and compassion for all, you will attract more love, happiness, and abundance.

**"We are what we think. All that we are arises with our thoughts. With our thoughts we make the world."**

- Buddha

# The Shift

*"When I finally got out of my own way"*

**"When you dig a well, there's no sign of water until you reach it, only rocks and dirt to move out of the way. When you have removed enough; soon the pure water will flow."**

- Buddha

I never had the calling in my 20's to become a mother. It worried me; I thought I might not ever have children. Maybe that's because I was too busy in a career working 80 hours a week, and I just didn't know how to listen to the whispers of the universe. I was travelling and building a company, and children were just not on my radar.

I was briefly married in my mid-twenties to a nice man, but in the end we realized we were just not right for each other. I believe we rushed into it, and we were too young to make a decision as important as marriage at the age of 25. Our last year together was painful, knowing we were not right for each other and that this was not the person I should have children with, should I ever feel that calling.

I lived in fear most of the time, too scared and too worried about what others would think of me if I walked away. I didn't want to be branded by divorce at the age of 29; it's not something you want on your credentials. I mean, do you know how many forms ask you if you have ever been divorced? Way too many. I didn't want to check off that box, and I didn't want to feel like a failure.

I felt it was my fault because I came from a family of divorce (twice over), that somehow I carried this divorce gene that made me completely incapable of having a good marriage. I struggled and went through many nights alone, deeply in pain trying to figure out what to do.

One night I was alone at home, feeling so sad, so scared, and so empty—like a hollow vessel floating away somewhere in the middle of a vast ocean. I didn't know what to do, and I had no idea where I was going. I was getting out of my business I had built over five hard years. I was so very lost and had been for quite some time. I had been adrift for so long I feared there was no way I'd ever find my way home.

After what seemed like an eternity of sobbing my heart out, a greater power me pulled me to the floor. I got down next to my bed, put my head to the Earth, and just prayed. I had never done this before; not this way.

That night, I turned myself inside out and found strength inside me that I never knew I had. A major shift occurred, and a voice that wasn't my own was speaking to my heart; this had never happened to me before, not like this. I went to Catholic school and attended church for over 10 years, and God had never spoke to me this way. Or, perhaps He did, and I had just never listened.

A major wave of peace washed over me. It was like my mind and body had been numbed just enough for me to listen to my Soul. The peace and quiet did not scare me—that night it changed me. At the time, I did not know that I could always tap into this feeling of peace through meditation, but on that night I was introduced to the feeling, brought there by a power greater than myself.

I got up the next morning, packed my bags, got in my car, and drove to my father's home. He knew what was going on the moment I walked through the door. I didn't have to say a word. I just walked up to him and cried, while he hugged me and told me I was doing the right thing and that everything would be ok. Somehow, I knew he was right. I had no doubt.

Something shifted for me after that day. A major force of energy swept over and through me, giving me strength and replacing fear with love. I had let go of the fears of being on my own, my fears of abandonment.

Suddenly, for the first time in my 29 years, I felt I really knew who I was and what I wanted out of life. Something inside of me became peaceful and calm. I finally had the desire to feel on the inside, without being scared of what I saw. The exterior did not matter so much anymore. Layer upon layer of build up, accumulated over so many years, just started falling away, and the real me—my spirit, my inner being—was shining gloriously.

**"Strip away the layers and reveal your Soul . . . give yourself up and then you become whole."**

- Matisyahu

That night I had moved the rocks and dirt around me out of the way. Pure water washed over me, and my Soul began to flow. An extreme shift occurred in my life, and for me it was just the beginning of my journey toward enlightenment. I was a Lotus flower emerging from the muddy waters, ready to open each petal and my true self and radiate in the warmth of the sun. My jewel had come out of the petals, and all that lay in between me and the life of my dreams was one message, one golden rule to live by:

*Remove guilt and fear to operate out of pure love alone, and everything will be ok. Trust in letting God guide you through life – he will always hold your hand and carry you when you fall.*

This I know for sure.

**"When you dig a well, there's no sign of water until you reach it, only rocks and dirt to move out of the way. When you have removed enough; soon the pure water will flow."**

- Buddha

Everyone who walks a path of spiritual growth will encounter at least one major "shift" along the way, but most likely multiple shifts. My shift occurred before I began delving deeply into my spiritual self; in fact, it was the catalyst for my intense interest in spiritual and holistic betterment. This was not my only shift, just the first.

As every person is different, our "Aha" moments occur at different points in our journeys, and they take on many different forms. These defining moments can cause dramatic changes within us and within our lives, as a result. Do not be afraid of such change—you must be willing to embrace it if you are to continue along the path.

While dramatic turning points are certainly common among those attuning to their spirituality for the first time, subtler shifts that unfold over time are equally possible and equally powerful. Sometimes we may incur a major shift without realizing it, only understanding our growth once we look back at where we have been.

How we grow and when we grow really depends on where we are coming from and where we are heading. And that is all part of our own wonderful, unique journeys through this life.

# *Love*

**"We are here to love and to be loved- everything else is secondary."**

"If I speak in the tongues of men or of angels but do not have love, I am only a resounding gong or a clanging cymbal.

If I have the gift of prophecy and can fathom all mysteries and all knowledge, and if I have a faith that can move mountains, but do not have love, I am nothing.

If I give all I possess to the poor and give over my body to hardship that I may boast, but do not have love, I gain nothing.

Love is patient, love is kind. It does not envy, it does not boast, it is not proud. It does not dishonor others, it is not self-seeking, it is not easily angered, it keeps no record of wrongs.

Love does not delight in evil but rejoices with the truth.

It always protects, always trusts, always hopes, always perseveres."

CORINTHIANS 13: 1-7

*Everybody wants Love. Love is who we are. It doesn't come and go, and you cannot find it anywhere unless you first find it in yourself. When you operate out of love, you operate with ease. When you do not operate from a place of Love, this creates dis~ease.*

Love is all you need. Once you realize the power and truth of this message, you understand the meaning of life. You understand why we are here. Everything we do must come down to love. Everything.

When love is your ruler, when it guides your daily life, you allow your true inner self to lead you along the path you are meant to walk. Love becomes your inner guidance system, magically moving you to the places you need to go and bringing you to the people you are meant to meet. Love frees you of hate, fear, jealousy, and envy.

The love feeling has a frequency vibration associated with it that is 500 Hz per second or above. The higher the vibrational frequency of our mind/body field the more spiritually evolved our life and our love are. It is our conscious thoughts that release the transmitters/hormone called oxytocin in the instance of loving thoughts.

When you operate out of love, your energy vibrates at a higher level, resonating with and attracting other forms of love on the same level. You also begin to exhibit a host of other virtues, almost entirely automatically. You become grateful, kind, sympathetic, giving, creative, passionate, peaceful, happy—these come with the package of love.

## Love vs. Guilt

We all have our Karma to deal with, from this and previous lifetimes; things we have already done cannot be changed. There are events and situations from our past that we have to endure (and oftentimes repeat) until we learn the lesson and move forward toward enlightenment. Nothing that happens to you is a mistake.

You have to dig deep to do the work and rid yourself of this Karma—that's the difficult part. If you keep acting in a destructive manner toward others, the environment, and yourself, then you have not healed, and you will not evolve.

Guilt is a wasted emotion. If you are doing something wrong and it is out of order, then change your behavior and your thought patterns. It's that simple.

Unfortunately, guilt is controlled by the ego, and the ego doesn't let you get off that easy. The ego-self is a "give me" machine. Whether it wants money, pleasure, people's approval, or control, the ego always strives to acquire things. And it always requires punishment. The ego feeds on negativity to keep you stuck because it can only grow when you are spiritually stagnant.

Guilt is an emotion that comes up around thoughts of the hurt and pain we have caused others, of our inability to protect loved ones from hurt, or of others' expectations of us that have gone unfulfilled. Guilt is also the ego's way of saying, "Look at all of the bad things I have done and the good things I haven't done. I'm no good, and I don't deserve any happiness." Guilt is an illusion that feeds the ego and keeps it alive. This absolutely wasted emotion keeps us acting out in negative ways and creates a cycle of abuse inside of us.

Women and mothers seem especially hard-wired with guilt—it's the most troublesome emotion we let envelop us. Guilt is that voice in the back of your head telling you that you're a lazy mom, that you can't be happy, that you spend too much time on yourself and not enough time with your kids. It's the voice that nags at you for yelling at your children when they test your patience beyond the limit.

Most mothers hold onto guilt, believing that releasing guilt means that they aren't sorry for whatever it is they did or did not do. The release of guilt does not negate love and caring, nor does holding on to guilt make love more powerful or meaningful. Guilt is a roadblock on the path to happiness and fulfilment. It builds emotional barriers to enlightenment out of events and situations that are actually learning opportunities for the spirit; situations that are meant to advance us on our paths.

There is no room in your life for guilt. If you live your life buried in guilt, dealing out punishment to yourself, then your children and loved ones will feel the pain of you not being fully available to them as your happy and authentic self. Guilt will weigh you down, literally dragging you through life, and you will miss everything.

God does not live in guilt—He lives in love. If you keep looking back, living in guilt, you will never move forward and live in the love that God offers. Get rid of guilt and replace it with taking responsibility, forgiving yourself, making amends, and accepting that certain circumstances are beyond your control. Give your energy to those things. And to love. God gives us second chances all the time, so learn your lessons and move on.

## Letting Go of Guilt

Guilt insinuates itself into our lives by masquerading as love, when in reality it is nearly the exact opposite. If you are used to operating out of guilt, it can be difficult to identify and separate from love. It helps to listen to your body.

Love feels like warmth radiating from your heart chakra. What does guilt feel like? Watch out for a twisting or gnawing sensation in your gut, accompanied by a tugging sensation within your chest. This is literally your ego sucking the love energy out of our chest and redirecting it for its own selfish purpose. The old saying, "tugging at your heart strings" pretty much sums it up.

Learn to use these sensations as cues for when guilt is taking over and masquerading as love. Identify whatever thoughts are going through your mind at that moment, and replace them with constructive, positive thoughts that come from a place of love.

## Loving Yourself

Loving yourself is the most essential prerequisite to living your best life. When you feel great about who you are, you radiate pure, magnetic energy that attracts the right things into your life. Moreover, taking time to address your needs can help you be a better loved one to family and friends. Do not feel guilty about making your foundation as strong as it needs to be to better care for the ones you love.

Most of us fall into the routine and behavioral pattern of making sure the important people and our children are taken care of while we neglect ourselves. When you put yourself first and make it a priority to put your basic needs ahead of everything else, you will have more energy and more love to give to others. When you tend to yourself and ensure that your foundations are firm, you feel healthy, beautiful, and balanced. You have the emotional strength to both take on the world and care for your loved ones.

**"You can search throughout the entire Universe for someone who is more deserving of your love and affection than you are yourself, and that person is to be found nowhere. You yourself, as much as anybody in the entire Universe deserve your love and affection."**

- Buddha

# *There Are Signs Everywhere*

"Serendipity. Look for something, find something else, and realize that what you've found is more suited to your needs than what you thought you were looking for."

- Lawrence Block

Ever since I can remember I have always looked at the world through creative binoculars and as if the living Earth was one beautiful giant treasure hunt. Anyone that knows me well can testify that I spend a lot of my time looking around for signs. I believe that our spirit guides, angels, loved ones who have passed on, and of course, the Divine, send little and sometimes big signs here on Earth to help guide us on our way.

My great aunt and godmother, who was much like a grandmother to me, passed away at 84 years old on the day after my daughter's first birthday. Aunt Cath was a devout Catholic, and we often spoke about Heaven at church when I was growing up. When it was her time to pass on we made a pact on her hospital bed that when she crossed over to the other side (Heaven) she would send me a sign to let me know that she was around. I told her that one of my favorite numbers was 11 and that when pennies appear in serendipitous places they could be "Pennies from Heaven." She laughed and gave me a smirk letting me know it was a deal.

It has been six and half years since she passed, and there is not a week that goes by without her sending me signs or messages. I always find a penny and a dime together on the ground (which equals 11 cents). Whenever I am thinking of her the song that played at her funeral (Sarah McLaughlin's "In the Arms of the Angel") comes on the radio.

The most amazing thing she ever did was appear to me in my home. I was taking pictures of our living room for the listing agent when we decided to sell our home, and after taking a few photos I picked the best one and uploaded it to my computer. Right in the middle of the photo was a very large orb of light. I zoomed in on it on my computer, and inside this orb of energy was her beautiful smiling face. I almost fell off my chair. I had always been able to feel the energy, but I had never seen it before.

I once read that when your spirit moves to heaven, you are operating at a faster, higher frequency. To understand this in a simple way, look at a ceiling fan. When it is not in motion you can see the blades. When you turn it on high speed, the blades are moving so fast they disappear. The blades are still there; you just can't see them because of the speed.

After this experience, I knew without a doubt not only that there is life after death, but also that our loved ones who pass on are around us when we ask them to be. They are there to guide us when we need them most. My Aunt Cath often tickles my hair. This is common for spirits to do—it feels like a tingling sensation on the head. This is their spiritual energy connecting with your spiritual energy.

During a recent trip to Turks and Caicos with my family, I was talking to my Aunt Cath a lot, asking her to guide me and keep me motivated and inspired to finish this book. We were sitting at the airport at the end of the trip, and a flood of information came pouring into my head at 6:30am. I could not write fast enough to get everything on paper.

Those in the creative industry know that when a burst of inspiration strikes, you have to take action. I said to my husband, "I'm sure my guides and my Aunt Cath are channelling me right now because I don't know where all of this information is coming from." I immediately started looking around for a sign.

Although I know my Aunt Cath and my Nana are around me on a regular basis, my heart so misses seeing them both in the physical world. But I do know without a doubt that both of them are with me on this journey of discovery, healing, and inspiring others. Beyond that, I know I will see them again one day.

On the flight out of Turks and Caicos I sat down next to a lovely lady, and we talked for what seemed like hours about our love of travel, the different places we have been in the world, and new places we still want to explore. I felt like I had known this lady my whole life. She seemed so familiar to me, but I knew that we had never met before.

When we landed in Miami, I hugged her and asked her name. She smiled at me and said, "I'm Cath." Chills ran down my body. She even looked like my Aunt Cath, too. They had the same nose and hair; it was unbelievable. There was my sign. Signed, sealed and delivered from the heavens.

I'm on the lookout for serendipity and magic all the time. For the past 17 years of my life, the number 406 has appeared to me when I know that I am on the right path. I even named my Creative Agency POTION406. White angelic feathers have floated by my window while writing this book, and just when I thought I had nothing else to say, I would find things and see things that inspired me to continue writing. When you believe in miracles and signs, the Universe will send you information on a daily basis to guide you. There are no coincidences. This is serendipity in work.

I have so many stories like this that I could write a book on signs alone. The amazing thing is that every time I witness serendipity at work, I am still in awe, like a kid in a giant candy store. When you are open, when you believe, anything and everything becomes possible in this world.

I am not the only one privy to signs and serendipitous moments, and psychics and mediums don't hold a monopoly on the ability to tune in, either. We all have a sixth sense and the gift to see signs that help guide us though life. You just have to learn to look and listen with your heart, not just your eyes. And believe.

The next time you think that something is a coincidence, think again. When you smell the perfume or cream of a loved one that has passed, believe that they are near you. When you see a name or number that relates to something in your life in an unusual place, believe this is a guide.

## *Painting Your Life Canvas by Number*

We all have our favorite numbers. They may be the date your children were born, your birthday or anniversary, the street number of the house that you grew up in, or even just a random number that appeals to you for no particular reason. We play the lotto with these numbers and make other gambles in life with them. In this digital age, we are literally surrounded by numbers at all times.

Numerology is the study of numbers. If you believe in the power of numbers, that the dates and times you do certain things have significance, then you can use numbers as signs to help manage and guide your life.

I love the number 8 because it represents a flowing infinity, wealth, and abundance. I always see 11:11 on the clock and make a wish, paying special attention to my surroundings at that time to see if that sequence of numbers is signalling something. 40 is a spiritual number to me that represents change. After 40 days of practicing anything consciously, it will become part of your life effortlessly. You hear this all throughout the Bible, as many tests from God were carried out over 40 days. I started this book just a few weeks after my 40th birthday.

My favorite number is 406. In my early twenties a friend of mine loved the number, and so I put it onto a t-shirt design as part of my fashion label, PH. My first collection made it into Nordstrom's department stores and the t-shirt sold out several times over across the nation. For the past 17 years I have seen the number 406 in the most serendipitous places, at the most opportune times. The chance of seeing this specific combination of numbers is rare, but I see it all the time.

If I am driving and trying to make a decision on something, I will see 406 on a sign or on a license plate. I often happen to look at the clock at exactly 4:06, at which point I pay attention to my thoughts and surroundings. I believe this number is a signal from my guides and angels who are showing me signs on Earth to guide me on my way.

For you, a different set of numbers will resonate with your energy. You may have a series of numbers that is special to you for no reason at all—maybe you just like the way they look or feel. Make sure the number combination is something unusual enough to stand out (three digits is a good rule of thumb but by no means a requirement).

Set your intention to make this your number guide and sign, and start paying close attention to your surroundings in your day-to-day life. The magic and miracle comes when your numbers start showing up at the most auspicious times, such as when you've just asked an important question or when you are wondering if you are doing the right thing.

You can certainly set your intentions with signs other than numbers (symbols, words, objects, or anything that has special significance to you), but numbers are a very easy place to start.

The Universe is a giant jigsaw puzzle, and every moment of your life is a piece. When you believe in the Divine, when you understand that we are all here on a path to discovery, the pieces of your puzzle will start to appear before your very eyes. When you go through your everyday life like you are living your own story, you realise that you can write your own script.

**"The best way to predict your future is to create it."**

- Abraham Lincoln

# *Healing*

**"The wound is the place where the Light enters you."**

- Rumi

Three years ago, I found myself in the midst of a terribly low period of my life. After the birth of my son, I fell into a cycle of anxiety, fear, and anger as I struggled, unsuccessfully, to walk away from a life situation that no longer served me.

Out of respect for my family, I will keep the details of that story private; they were difficult and trying circumstances for all of us, to say the least. How I reached that dark and lonely place is less important than how I found my way back.

Depressed and anxious, I felt the heavy burdens of other people's problems—other people's karma—squeezing the life out of me. As joyful as my daughter and newborn son made me, I felt the overwhelming pull of dead weight dragging me down. All I wanted was a peaceful, happy life, and yet an epic saga of invasive drama continued on with new chapters and bizarre twists. Try as I might to smile and persevere, the barrage was seriously taking its toll.

I was stuck, and no amount of positive thinking could get me out of what I was doing to myself. I believed whole-heartedly that the situation was out of my hands, out of my control; I had convinced myself that it was not my fault. After all, you cannot control the actions of others.

I was in such a void that one night I grabbed my computer and searched the Internet desperately for a healer who could help lift the bad energy that had seeped into my life from outside sources. When I called to book the appointment at midnight, knowing I would be leaving a voicemail, the desperation in my voice must have rung out loud and clear. She called me the next morning at 7:30am and asked, "Can you get here today?" I literally ran to my car to get there.

When I arrived at her office she took one look at me said, "Your aura is so brown." I knew this was true, not because I could see it but because I felt it. The ominous cloud I had been living in was real—it was my aura, dark and heavy like a giant ball of dirty smoke spiralling around my being. It was so thick at times that I couldn't breathe. This was not who I was; I had never in my life allowed other people to affect me in this way. And yet, this time I had.

My therapist, Farah, was a trained counsellor but also practiced a method of energy repair known as Pranic Healing. Pranic Healing works on your meridians, internal organs, chakras, and aura to remove "used up" or diseased energy and replace it with fresh, vital energy. The meaning of the word "dis-ease" is simple: your body's natural state of ease is disrupted, and the resulting imbalance causes mental and physical illness.

Pranic Healing was developed by Master Choa Kok Sui, who also authored the book, Miracles Through Pranic Healing. Master Choa's method of energy healing goes a lot deeper than traditional Reiki, using your own Prana (Pranic energy or "Vital Life Source") to heal you.

What I have come to learn over all my years working with energy healers is that all your ailments exist energetically before they manifest themselves physically or psychologically.

When I sat down across from Farah and began to explain the recent events of my life, I expected her to validate my pain as the product of great injustice. I wanted her to say, "You poor thing, how could this person have done this to you? I feel so bad that you have been driven to this place. Poor thing. Why you?" I wanted her to affirm that I was a victim of circumstance and recognize the strength it took for me to remain standing on my own two feet.

Nothing could have prepared me for what she said instead. She looked directly into my eyes and stated plainly, "You have allowed this in your life. You are responsible for your situation, for the state you're in." I was stunned, like a deer in headlights.

My brain fumbled to process her words. Had I had heard her correctly? The fog of shock quickly burned away as an acrid column of rising anger took hold. How could she say such a thing? I had trusted this woman with very personal details of a story that caused me great pain. I had come to her seeking reassurance and healing, but she didn't understand me at all. This was not my fault! Someone else was causing me heartache and grief, and it was all I could do to keep it together. She obviously hadn't listened to a single word I had said.

Farah never broke eye contact as she waited for a response. I looked at her, feeling lost and betrayed. In so little time, I had invested so much hope in her ability to help me. She was supposed to help me open the door to recovery, or at the very least a window that would let some light and fresh air into my life. Instead, I had been talking to a wall.

"Uh no," I finally managed with an edge of thinly veiled irritation. "I think you heard me wrong. The person I've been talking about for the last 40 minutes—that's who did this to me."

Her gaze sharpened and her voice softened as she replied, "You have allowed yourself to be in this person's way, in their business, and a part of their life. You know what to expect from this situation. It seems to me that the one thing you can count on is that involvement with this person will cause you grief and disappointment time after time. And, yet, you are still there waiting for this person to change. Why? Why are you subjecting yourself to the misery? Why let their energy and aura control your life? This is your doing."

The light bulb went off with the brightest flash of wisdom I had ever experienced. I had let all of this happen—I had allowed it. I had remained in a situation well past its expiration date, fighting against the lesson I was meant to learn. I realized in that moment that if I had only listened to my intuition screaming at me, if I had only paid attention to the signs right in front of my face, I could have walked away gracefully a long time ago.

Farah must have seen the realization dawning in my eyes. She knew that I was ready to hear what she had to say next. She continued candidly, "Stop trying to fix people. Stop playing that role. Allow this person to walk their own path through life. If they are going to make mistakes, then that's their business, their karma, and their role—not yours. It isn't possible to help people who aren't willing to help themselves, and it's not your responsibility to heal them or fix them if they don't want to do the work."

I got it—I really got it and the guilt lifted.

I had been so conditioned from childhood, after my parents' divorce, to be the pillar of the family. I was the family "fixer," the person who worked to solve problem after problem so that we could live a somewhat normal and happy life. For over 30 years this had been my role in my very complex family structure. I had never wavered from this responsibility that I had taken upon myself, as the guilt would be a burden far too heavy to carry.

Why would I abandon my duties to my own family, when I knew firsthand what it felt like to feel abandoned and alone inside? Why would I want or allow anyone else to feel that when I could try to do something about it? But something inside of me changed that day, as suddenly as the simple flip of a switch in my head.

*That day I discovered that you can love and give unconditionally to someone, but you don't have to give up yourself in the process.*

You should never deny yourself your God-given rights of love, peace, and happiness. Sometimes you just have to let go and let people figure out their own lives, walk their own paths, and face their own struggles. Love will always find its way back to you when it is ready—love always finds a way.


**"Do not let the behavior of others destroy your own inner peace."**

-Dalai Lama XIV


That two-hour session with Farah changed my life. She was like an angel sent to me as the guide I needed to get me back on my path here on Earth. She had helped me open the door, after all. When I walked out of her clinic, the sun was shining, and for the first time in a very long time, I felt its warmth on my skin. I was in awe of the pure blue sky above me and the beauty of all the trees around me. I was breathing, and I was awake! I woke up to myself that day, deciding that I didn't want to feel like that anymore, not ever again. So I changed.

I knew for sure that my Nana, who had just passed on a little over a year before, had been the one guiding me to the healer that day. I got in my car and sat in the happy, quiet, meditative aura that I had created. The peace, love and gratitude I finally felt was overwhelming.

I looked at the car parked in front of mine and the license plate number read—LYN 406. Lyn was my Nana's name, and 406 is the number I see whenever the Universe reassures me that everything is ok and that I am on the right path. The message could not have been clearer: she was the one who guided me there to help me heal. Without a shadow of a doubt, I knew that I had been carried there that day by the arms of an angel, or in my case, many angels.

I drove around the city for two hours that day after my healing, happier than I had been in a long time. I laughed uncontrollably as I drove through the city tunnels and along the river, taking in all the beauty that the world has to offer for our pleasure.

The sun shone that day like it always did, but it seemed like a whole new sun and a whole new world to me. I had finally gotten out of my own way (again) and removed the shadow that I had cast over my own life. Alive again and ready to take on the world, I was no longer a victim. That day I became a powerful warrior woman, and I knew that the path I was about to walk down was going to be bright.

"As my sufferings mounted I soon realized that there were two ways in which I could respond to my situation -- either to react with bitterness or seek to transform the suffering into a creative force. I decided to follow the latter course."

- Martin Luther King Jr.

# *Enlightenment*

**"There are two ways of spreading light: to be the candle or the mirror that reflects it."**

- Edith Wharton

Buddhists believe that true Enlightenment ends the spirit's cycle of reincarnation here on Earth. When there is nothing left to learn, when all darkness has been extinguished from every corner of your Soul, and when all of your karmic debts have been paid, backwards and forwards, then you have achieved true Enlightenment. Your Soul goes to Nirvana to become One with the Universe.

Buddhist tradition also says that sometimes Souls who have achieved true Enlightenment choose to return to Earth anyway; although they may not have anything left to learn, there is plenty for them to teach. If this is true, then the Dalai Lama is certainly one of those Souls.

Whenever we learn a lesson, whenever we shed another layer, we move closer to ultimate Enlightenment. We reach Nirvana only at the end of a very, very long journey, but we are always moving toward it, and we can all achieve degrees of enlightenment here on Earth.

Enlightenment cannot really be explained, only experienced. It is a lot like love—nobody can really tell you what it is like, but when you find and feel it you know. Enlightenment is a lot like love because, in fact, it is love. Love of life, love of self, love of all. You become aware of others beings and start to look for the beauty in all people and things.

Enlightenment very literally means exactly what it says—you become full of light. The light is inside each and every one of us, burning brighter than a million suns. You need only to look at a newborn baby to know that this is true. The more we learn and grow, the brighter that light becomes.

Sometimes we get lost and forget our Soul's true purpose. Sometimes we let dark shadows in to obscure the light. However dim it may grow, the light is never extinguished. It's always right there, hiding behind the layers that pile up over the years. When you remove the layers to seek your True Self, the reward is Enlightenment.

After you work to break through your internal barriers, after you have rid yourself of all anger and fear, you live with vitality and spirit. When you stop seeking and simply let go, you learn to go with the flow and experience who you really are. Love, peace, and gratitude rule your world. Heaven becomes Earth.

Enlightenment is also a personal journey, between you and God. The beauty of awakening is that it is an ongoing process of ever-greater awareness; the more light you let in, the brighter you become.

When your heart and Soul beat and expand out of your chest, when you feel happiness like you were when you were a child, you will know the surface has been cracked and that the light is shining.

**"Enlightenment is ego's ultimate disappointment"**

- Chögyam Trungpa

# My Personal OM Formula

## noun \'ōm pill\

A pill of life loaded with OM—ultimate reality. Completely natural. Made up of: the Divine, love, gratitude, happiness, prayer, Yoga, meditation, forgiveness, music, mindful breathing, and too many other ingredients to list.

**Taken daily, it causes utter bliss:** The Universe has an unlimited supply to prescribe, but is only be effective if you live from the inside out.

A lot of women have approached me over the years to ask me, "How do you do it? How are you always happy and juggling your family, life, a busy career, lots of friends, a husband, two children, and travel, yet still have enough time to take care of you? Truth is, there are moments my life is not so Zen at all, when I lose it and disconnect from my authentic self.

There have been days, weeks, and months that I stopped practicing my spiritual and holistic formula, and through this time I suffered. I was lost, empty, and in pain for far too long; longer than necessary to learn the lesson. Or perhaps it was simply longer than I'd hoped—we all take as long as we need to walk our own path.

My personal spiritual formula has seen many incarnations in its evolution over the years; it is a continual work in progress because life is a continual work in progress. I work on myself, I study the wisdoms and traditions from cultures around the world, and I find new things that bring me joy and nourish my Soul.

This section contains many of the essential ingredients in my formula for happiness and fulfilment in everyday life. It is the simple things, in addition to the immense love I have for myself, my husband, my children, my family, and my friends that get me through life.

This is my "OM Tonic," which connects me to my spirit and allows me to live and breathe the purest, most holistic life I can.

Take comfort in the simple pleasures of life—the small gifts from the Divine—and you will live and breathe as you never have before.

# Inhale ~ Exhale

# Just Breathe

**Learn the art of sipping the air.**

**Fully abundant and there for your pleasure.**

**The sweet nectar of life.**

**Close your eyes. Inhale ~ Exhale**

## Inhale ~ Exhale

A shell to the ear, the sound of a breath
A whisper, a feather
That separates us from death

A leaf dancing down a flowing stream
A peaceful, ethereal, floating dream
A rolling wave on a sandy shore
A swooping bird about to soar

The fuel for life, a connection to peace
A link from the heavens
Endless
While on this Earth will never cease

A Mindful breath
A drink of life
That cuts through fear and anxiety
Through tension like a knife
A blessed reminder from the divine above
A pure white wind on the wings of a dove

Close your eyes and begin to soar
and you will live and breathe,
as you never have before.

Breath is the Divine's gift to us. Conscious, mindful breath is the most important ingredient in your life's spiritual formula. When you breathe consciously you make yourself available to life—you become fully present. When you are present you are truly living.

Before you journey into this section, I want you to practice this OM For The Mom Breath Meditation. Experience is the best way to understand the true power of breath.

**Want to feel high on life? Then learn how to breathe.**

## *Breath Meditation*

First, put down the book, close your eyes, and either lay down in Shavasana—on your back—or stay seated in a comfortable meditative pose with your legs crossed and hands resting on your knees. Make sure your surroundings are quiet, and breathe deeply in and out of your nose for 40 breaths. Count silently in your mind while focusing solely on a white lotus flower in your mind's eye and nothing else. When you're done, sit quietly and continue reading on the power of mindful breath.

## Inhale ~ Exhale

## *The Power of The Breath*

Breath—the all-important, life giving elixir. Without any conscious effort on our part, our hearts beat, our stomachs digest, and our lungs breathe. Of all our vital functions, however, breath is special in that we have the ability to consciously control it whenever we choose. This is the key to mastery over our physical bodies.

One of the Five Principles of Yoga is Pranayama, which promotes proper breathing. Correct breathing in Yoga—and in life—delivers more oxygen to the blood and to the brain, allowing for control of the

Prana, also known as the vital life energy. The union of Pranayama and Asana (Yoga poses) is considered the highest form of purification and self-discipline.

When we are scared or nervous, we cannot will our hearts to beat slower, but we can will our lungs to breathe slowly, deeply, and effectively. And this breath, in turn, slows down the beating of our hearts.

Anxiety is an ailment that stems from our bodies' biological "fight-or-flight" response to perceived threats. The fight-or-flight response evolved as a means of responding to potentially life-threatening situations, such as predators, in an instant. Part of that response involves an increased heart rate and an automatic shift in breathing patterns—long, deep breaths that expand into the stomach become shallow, rapid breaths that stay in the chest. This automated switch in breath is designed to pump more oxygen and blood to our muscles, in case we need to run for our lives or fend off an attack.

The threats we perceive in the modern world tend to be far less physical—running from a predator vs. paying our bills on time—so the fight-or-flight response works against us in most stressful situations. When inordinate stress builds up over time, with no physical threat to respond to, we are left with a keyed-up nervous system, tightness in the chest, and no outlet for the fight-or-flight response. This can wreak havoc on our bodies.

Identifying anxiety and correcting restricted breathing patterns is the simplest step toward a happy and healthy life. Focused and mindful breathing in through the nose, out through the nose, and into the belly is like taking the most relaxing pill you could ever imagine, without the side effects of dulled senses and disconnection. Far from it. You become more connected, more aware, and more alive. Breath is the backbone and foundation of all your practice into becoming the peaceful, warrior woman you want to be.

A recent study found that breathing exercises, Yoga, meditation, and prayer all have the ability to invoke the body's "relaxation response," which is the opposite of the fight-or-flight response. There is hard scientific proof that these practices bring you into a state of well-being. [1]

The study found that these effects go all the way down to your genes, switching gene expression that invokes a stress response for gene expression that favors a relaxation response. Essentially, they change the way that you and your body respond to stressful situations, making you a more relaxed and healthier human being. Wow.

[1] Dusek JA, Otu HH, Wohlhueter AL, Bhasin M, Zerbini LF, et al. (2008) Genomic Counter-Stress Changes Induced by the Relaxation Response. PLoS ONE 3(7): e2576. doi:10.1371/journal.pone.0002576

## Find Some Breathing Space

*Find and create a sanctuary that resonates with your Soul. Find some breathing space for your spirit.*

Creating a meditation space in your home or office is a wonderful way to escape in your day-to-day life. You can close your eyes and quiet your mind anytime throughout your day. You can literally take a mini vacation—through yourself, to yourself—to nourish your Soul with pure tranquillity every day.

I allow myself as many of these "Breathing Space Journeys" as my mind needs. Some days it seems all I do is breathe to get myself through life's challenges and chaos.

As you breathe in, pay attention to this simple act that makes you fully aware, fully alive. This will bring you joy and harmony. When you learn to focus on your breath, you stop thinking. Imagine the lotus flower opening beautifully to the morning sun—it does so effortlessly - this is how your breath should be.

When you are ready for the next step, a true escape and to return to the calm center within yourself, you can turn your Breathing Space Journeys into meditation sessions. (See the Meditation chapter for more information.)

As a busy woman / mother your life will become stressed—this is inevitable. Mindful breathing penetrates into every fibre of your being to center, calm, and strengthen your mind, body, and spirit.


A fire is not put out with the energy of more fire; it is contained and put out with the flow and energy of water.

## *Let Your Space Breathe*

Just as the free and natural flow of oxygen is vital for bodily health, the free and natural flow of energy in the space you occupy is vital for mental and spiritual health.

Feng Shui (Feng means wind and Shui means water) is the ancient art and science of how to balance the energy of a space or environment in order to bring health, wealth, and happiness to the people occupying it.

It is extremely important to make sure that your home and work environments have good energy—chi—flowing through them at all times to keep your life in balance.

> ~ De-clutter and clean your home and office. This is Rule Number One! Simplify your life and get rid of extraneous possessions so that good energy can flow freely throughout the environment.

> ~ Make sure there are no dead flowers or dried potpourri around you—their dead energy will pollute your space. Bring in money trees to attract wealth. Keep green plants and fresh flowers to bring vital, positive chi into your life.

> ~ Smudge your space at least once a week with sage. You can buy sage smudging sticks at Whole Foods or from many online stores. Burning sage removes trapped and negative energy from your space.

> ~ Decorate your home with colors, pictures, and anything you love that makes you feel happy. Add art and photos of your loved ones and travel experiences, as well as images that make you feel fresh, alive, and creative. My home and office are full of Buddha statues, Indian Goddess statues, my own art, candles, incense, aromatherapy oils, positive quotes, cotton throws, meditation altars, fresh flowers, and chimes.

~ Put together a visualization board of what you want to achieve in your life. Hang this up somewhere visible so that you can see your dream every day, right before your eyes. My visualization board has a picture of the Om for the Mom book cover with "New York Times Best Seller" printed on the top. Next to that is a photo of Oprah's Harpo Studios. It also has a photo of what my dream Om Philosophy retreat looks like in the Caribbean. My photos of my loved ones are the most prevalent and act as a permanent display of the things that are most important in my life.

~ Figure out where your money corner is in both your home and your office. For 2013, it is the northeast corner of your environment. Place something heavy in this corner, such as an urn, a statue, or a heavy Buddha. Place a money tree in the same corner, a dish with coins in it, and a note to the Universe stating what successes you want to achieve. Finally, add a citrine stone to attract wealth.

I recently set up the money area in a friend's office space to get the energy flowing in her environment. One hour after I left the office, the phone began ringing off the hook. She received four large orders that she had been waiting on for three months, and two clients that owed her a lot of money called to say they had checks ready for her to pick up.

~ Add wind chimes at the front and back entries of your home/office to bring in good energy.

~ Print out a Bagua Map (you can find one on the Internet) to figure out the map of your home of office. This will show you where to put certain crystals, water features, and other energy enhancing tools.

Positive energy goes where positive energy flows.

ༀ་མ་ཎི་པ་དྨེ་ཧཱུྃ།

# *Yoga*

**"Yoga is a journey of the self,
Through the self
To the self."**


- Bhagavad Gita

For me, there is nothing like Yoga to connect the mind, body, and spirit with power and grace. Yoga teaches you to be present. When you practice Yoga, you open up a connection to something greater than yourself. This practice is one of the world's most ancient technologies for establishing and maintaining optimal health and well-being in these bodies of ours. I cannot hope to understand or explain the depths of its mysteries, but I can tell you about how it makes me feel, how it has changed my life, and how it can change yours.

I have been practicing Yoga for over 12 years now, and every day I still learn more and more about what it can teach me. When my Soul became fully aware—the day I let the sun shine onto the shadows that I had cast over my own life—that was the day the world became more beautiful. Not long after that I literally fell onto a Yoga mat, and from that day on I knew this practice had to be part of my life. I soon figured out that Yoga empowers me to create a world that I can transform. When I get on my mat, my private sanctuary, I turn dreams into reality and live large in a small, sacred space.

Yoga has become such an important thread in my life, and I know that I can't live without it. The discipline of the practice has given me immense internal strength, and I attribute at least 80% of my spiritual and personal growth to Yoga and meditation. Without either, I don't think I would be here on this path. Actually, I know that I wouldn't.

In the Western world we are so caught up in all the wrong things, and we make life more complicated than it really is. Everywhere you look there are so many people who are disconnected from the Source. People are really in a mess. I mean really and truly in a mess. So many people chase the wrong things—fame, money, power, and possessions. Too many people continue to look outside themselves for happiness and validation, all the while knowing that the money, the material possessions, the latest job promotion, the shopping, the alcohol, and the drugs are not filling that empty space. This way of living eventually catches up with you. No matter how much you feed the ego with Earthly possessions, they will certainly never make you happy.

Your authentic self is a radiantly simple being who doesn't need material things to be happy. You have to go within and find your true self to discover how easy happiness really is. Yoga is one of many methods that can take you to that place inside; it has an almost magical ability to bring calm in the midst of chaos.

The world we live in is a projection of our own thoughts, and our perspective equals our experience of reality. Yoga is so liberating because it strips everything away, letting you clear your mind and discover bliss. It supplies you with all the happiness you need. When you incorporate Yoga into your life you will find that you won't need to accumulate so many material things—the more you practice the less you need.

## Life is not out there, life is in you.

There is so much anxiety and stress surrounding us all, meeting us at every turn, but Yoga is a refuge. When you get on that mat something truly magical happens; you enter a sacred space where you can open your heart and awaken your Soul. After you get off the mat you become clearer; a shift occurs and you start to function differently. If you work with your mind and your body (rather than against them, as modern life unwittingly trains us to do) you can finally make a shift in your life. What was once stuck will start to flow.

Yoga teaches you to be honest with yourself, and over time you will start to manage your life in a more productive and spiritual way. When you practice Yoga you will eventually feel a connection to the Divine; how strong that connection grows will depend on how far you let yourself go. In a very short amount of time you cannot only create a strong body, but also a calm mind, as well as an overall feeling of balance and good health.

When you connect with yourself and the Divine you become free. When you are free you can deal with all realms of your life. Fear, pain, self-doubt, and suffering live in the dark places in your body. Yoga lets the light in to shine on those dark crevices and bathes negative energy in golden positivity.

Yoga also shows you the flow and rhythm of life, and it teaches you how to follow it by connecting Asanas (poses) and movement through mindful breath. You move gracefully by following the flow of your breath, and you draw strength to hold and maintain difficult postures by digging deeply into the power of your breath.

Each pose has a specific purpose that delivers very specific results. There is a certain euphoria that happens during Drishti (focus poses), and when you move you do so in a very conscious way to keep your balance. Warrior poses develop tremendous strength of mind and body, teaching your body to remain calm while grounding you and connecting you firmly to the Earth.

When you follow the flow of your breath and energy through your body you connect to the flow of life. When you let go of all the dark stuff you will radiate love, harmony, gratitude, truth, and compassion.

## *Find Your Yoga*

I love that Yoga has become such a phenomenon in the Western world. Today you can find thousands upon thousands of studios everywhere, from the middle of bustling urban cities to small and quiet rural towns. Ten years ago, when I opened my Yoga, wellness, and spiritual day spa, Yoga was nowhere near as popular as it is today. It is great to see so many people trying to find their inner beauty and peace through this ancient practice and technology.

More and more people all over the world are falling into Yoga and meditation studios in desperation, trying to find a way to chip away at their outer shells and let the light in. I see it all the time in the classes I attend. Every time I see a new Soul sitting there afraid and alone, I always envision a ball of white light around them. I say to myself, "Half the battle was making the decision to get here on the mat in this sacred space to start doing the work. Bless you with lots of love and light, and may God give you the strength to keep coming, to do the work and find your bliss."

Yoga has changed a lot from its traditional practice to accommodate the more "fitness-minded" students in the Western world. As opposed to a fitness for your mind and spiritual strength, many Yoga classes focus on sculpting the body alone, with a perfunctory "Namaste" thrown in at the end as an afterthought.

Westernized Yoga classes can be little more than glorified fitness classes, so please choose your studio and your classes wisely. Yoga is not a sport. If your class gives you a killer body but doesn't also nourish your Soul, then you haven't been doing Yoga.

For me the environment, the energy, and the teacher all have to be in harmony for me to get the most out of my practice. I am so sensitive to energy that I need the whole package for it to connect with me. I personally love Yoga that brings in the traditional elements of incense, chanting, and meditation into the practice.

If you're new to Yoga, Hatha is a great place to start; it teaches you the physical poses and how to connect to the inner self. More advanced practices include: Vinyasa, Ashtanga, Bikram, Iyengar, Jivamukti and Kundalini. The beauty of Yoga is that it's a personal practice, and it's not uncommon to have beginners in a class with more advanced students. Yoga is not a competition, and a good teacher will offer up to three options for most poses in a class—beginner, intermediate, and advanced positions.

If you are looking for a sacred space to connect and start doing your work, focus more on smaller studios, not the practices in gyms and health clubs. They are great for exercising the body, but most don't go very deep into the philosophy of Yoga and meditation. A studio that heavily promotes meditation will most likely practice the traditional elements of this ancient technology. If you want intense spiritual work, envelope yourself in the practice of Kundalini or Jivamukti Yoga. They will almost certainly change your life.

I recently fell into a Jivamukti studio and instantly fell in love with this style of Yoga. It is very spiritual and true to the ancient practice, but there is also this magic about it that is truly special. My love for it also has a lot to do with the studio, and my teacher Robert, who focuses on making sure that all your senses are invigorated during your practice.

Robert's "Bali Spirit" class magically takes me away every time on a mini vacation to Bali – I am transported instantly with the scent of the oils, the Balinese chimes, music and the spiritual essence that only breathes and lives in Bali. If you have ever been to Bali, you will know the spiritual magic I am speaking of, which words simply can not describe. When the essence of the Balinese energy touches you, it is infused in your spirit. Robert creates a magical flow and fusion of Yoga and the essence of Bali and it is truly blissful.

*This is Yoga. This is how you find bliss in your daily life.*

These types of studios and teachers are what the essence of Yoga is all about. There is a magic in them and when you step in there miracles happen. You get transported, you carry that magic out of the studio into the world, and your life starts changing. It just makes your spirit soar and everything else just flows.

## JIVAMUKTI { JEE -VA -MOOK -TEE }

JIVA = Individual Soul/self   Mukti= Liberation

*Jivamukti Yoga* is a path to enlightenment through compassion for all beings. The method created by David Life and Sharon Gannon in New York City is grounded in the original meaning of the Sanskrit word asana as "seat, connection" - relationship to the Earth. Earth implies all of life. So the practice of asana becomes more than mere physical exercise to keep one's body fit or to increase strength or flexibility; it becomes a way to improve one's relationship to all others and thus lead to enlightenment and eternal happiness.

*Embrace the love of spiritual energy, and you will find your true, authentic self through Yoga and Meditation.*

*Yoga is more than the physical exercise; it is a love of spiritual energy mixed with the art of breath and movement.*

## *Kundalini Yoga*

After 12 years of practicing Yoga I found myself in a Kundalini class one day, and since then I have never looked back. Kundalini is one of the most authentic, most holistic forms of Yoga I have ever practiced. I fell in love with Kundalini Yoga the day I sat and chanted my first mantra in a class. I literally felt like I was high on life. My first thought was, "I want more people, especially women and mothers to taste this so they can incorporate it into their lives."

I have been so blessed to connect with guides and teachers over the years through my different Yoga practices, but more than all others Kundalini makes my spirit really soar. It is my own personal connection to myself and to the Divine. My teacher, Karampal Kaur, has the gift to take you on a journey, helping transport your mind and body to another place. She has taught me to go within and to feel at peace in the void.

The word Kundalini is derived from a Sanskrit word Kundal, which means "coiled up." Kundalini is believed to be an innate, dormant energy resting in the base of the spine inside the Sacrum.

The purpose of Kundalini Yoga is to awaken the Kundalini energy and nourish the tree of life within us. Kundalini Yoga is supposed to be the supreme of all Yoga and the one closest to the original and sacred form of Yoga developed over 2,000 years ago. Guru Vashistha said that Kundalini is the seat of absolute knowledge. When Kundalini energy is distributed through the body it awakens and feeds all seven chakras in the body with the vital energy that they need to function optimally in our bodies.

The following tells the story of Kundalini through the beautiful words of Karampal Kaur, one of my spirit guides and teachers who has brought a whole new dimension to my practice and giving me the light to become a teacher. For her I am eternally grateful—*Namaste*.

## *Transformational Mantras & Meditations of*

## *Kundalini Yoga*

Kundalini Yoga Mantras and Meditations come from the highly respected teachings of spiritual teacher Yogi Bhajan, a master of Kundalini Yoga who delivered authentic Kundalini Yoga to the modern world in the late 60's. He made these once secret teachings available to all.

Kundalini Yoga is a life energy management system that uses all faculties of the body in harmony to awaken your Kundalini (your own natural vital energy) to elevate your consciousness and your human experience.

It contains powerful tools for clearing and restructuring the subconscious mind and includes various recipes of Asanas (body movement and postures), Mantra (strengthening the mind through repetition of positive affirmations), Mudras (hand positions that stimulate the nerve centre's of your brain), Pranayama (breath techniques), and Visualization.

Kundalini Yoga is a whole body and mind experience to restructure the way you process your thoughts, resulting in a truly deep and authentic feeling of peace. It is an effective catalyst for change, a proven ancient technology that anyone can experience.

Yogi Bhajan emphasized the importance of women, the divine feminine energy in society. His lifestyle teachings continue to have a profound effect on how thousands of truth seekers and yoginis choose to live their lives in nobility and grace.

The mantras and meditations at the end of each section of this book will help you walk this honorable path to self-discovery, spirituality, and your true identity.

~ Karampal Kaur

ༀ་མ་ཎི་པ་དྨེ་ཧཱུྃ།

I could write a book on Yoga and meditation alone, but describing their benefits really does you no good unless you are inspired to go out there and try these practices for yourself.

For those of you reading this book who are already practicing, try to remember to take Yoga off the mat and apply the Asanas, chants, mantras, and principles in your day-to day life.

Ultimately, your practice does not end on the mat. The more you practice Yoga; you realize that you can incorporate the benefits of these poses into your everyday life to handle anything life throws at you—(beyond increased physical strength to help you carry twice as many grocery bags and kids). Yoga facilitates mind-body awareness that you carry with you, helping you live in the moment and live your life with purpose, grace and intention.

**"Yoga is not a religion. It is a science, science of well-being, science of youthfulness, science of integrating body, mind and Soul."**

- Amit Ray (Yoga and Vipassana: An Integrated Life Style)

# *Meditation*

**"If you want to conquer the anxiety of life, live in the moment, live in the breath."**

- Amit Ray, Om Chanting and Meditation

"It takes a little time to create a gap between the witness and the mind. Once the gap is there, you are in for a great surprise, that you are not your mind, that you are the witness, a watcher."

- Osho

Imagine pouring yourself a glass of the purest, clearest spring water that ever existed. Now imagine scooping a few spoonfuls of dirt into the glass. Now stir. Stir until the dirt and water become one, and what you'll you have is a glass of brown, muddy water.

As long as you continue stirring and moving the water around, it will remain both agitated and murky. But stop stirring long enough to let the water settle entirely, and all of the dirt will eventually sink to the bottom. The rest of the water will become crystal clear once more.

This is how the mind works when you meditate. The spring water represents your mind in its natural state, and the dirt represents all of the input going in day after day. If we never take the time to stop thoughts and worries from churning through our heads, our minds become as murky as the water. Amidst the swirling muck, it is easy to lose perspective—up, down, left, or right become indistinguishable.

In today's hectic world, most of us end up "stirring" our brains on autopilot. After all, there is so much to think about and keep straight—the tasks at hand, our running "To Do" lists, the next deadline, scheduling time with friends and loved ones, our laundry lists of responsibilities, and debts owed, to say nothing of the endless electronic distractions that surround us at every waking moment. And that's before you become a mother.

Multitasking and multi-thinking have become the norm. What's more, so many of us end up spending our "me time" on the computer or watching TV. When we stimulate our brains non-stop, our brains forget even how to stop. Autopilot stirring.

The worst part about having a brain on autopilot is that we end up teaching ourselves to ignore the background thoughts running through our heads. We let our subconscious minds run wild like unsupervised children while focusing on the conscious tasks at hand.

Meditation retrains the brain to slow down and eventually enables you to clear your mind of all thoughts at will. Ah, peaceful silence! When you quiet the mind and stop the stirring you move all dirt and build up out of the way, and life becomes a whole lot clearer.

There are many different forms of meditation, and while the roots of meditation lie in spiritual growth and enlightenment, most people today use it as a tool for relaxation and stress relief. Meditation is a peaceful sanctuary in your mind where no racing thoughts barge in and where you take control of your life.

**"Watch your thoughts; they become words.**

**Watch your words; they become actions.**

**Watch your actions; they become habits.**

**Watch your habits; they become character**

**Watch your character; for it becomes your destiny."**

- Upanishads

When practiced consistently, meditation is nothing short of life changing. When you sit (or lie) down to meditate the goal is to have no goal, no intent. The way to meditation is in letting go and just trusting how powerful the process can be.

When there is no thought in your mind ~ that is meditation. The peaceful space between the thoughts ~ that is enlightenment. Tuning in to the present moment brings peace and well-being, and your energy begins vibrating at a different frequency. When you really delve deep into meditation, when you connect to yourself and everything around you in a place where time has no meaning, you float in euphoric bliss. You feel high. You feel truly alive.

While the very idea of meditating can be intimidating or even scary to those who have never practiced before, there is nothing to worry about. Meditation is a peaceful, positive, and unimaginably life-affirming practice, and you do not need special skills to do it. Meditation is for everyone. It requires only dedication, a desire for change, and a little patience.

When I started, I didn't think I could sit in meditation for long. I am a very energetic person by nature, and I have to really try hard to focus on one thing at a time. It was challenging at first, but after a few sessions my mind and body just slipped into the mode, automatically going into the very tranquil state that meditation brings about.

Your thoughts in meditation are just that—thoughts. When you train yourself to simply observe them as mind chatter that is not connected to your authentic self, you can learn to let them pass. Thoughts simply wash away when you acknowledge them without giving energy to them or judging them. I sometimes visualize putting a thought in a bottle and watching it float out to sea, past the horizon. I watch the thoughts disappear in a gentle, peaceful way. This visualization technique is wonderful for difficult energy that you are trying to remove from your mind and your life.

Meditation detoxes and cleanses your mind, clearing it to let all the beauty of the Universe flow in. You just have to learn to pause and find your breathing space in day-to-day life. Carve out five-minute breathing space moments as often as you can. Escape outside, to your home sanctuary, the bath, or the shower and just breathe. Close your eyes and breathe.

You have over 60,000 thoughts racing through your mind every day; can you imagine how exhausted it gets? A tired mind equals stress and anxiety. If you walk 60,000 steps, that's 30 miles. What would your body feel like if you did not sit down to take a break? Exhausted and run down. You have to take care of your mind; you have to let it rest. It is as important if not more valuable than your physical body.

When you meditate, you may stir up some negative energy and emotions. This is a good thing. We cannot run away from our fears in life—we must face them to heal them and move on. Stress and anxiety come when you are disconnected from your true, higher self, and clearing the path is the only way to be reunited with the real you. You are the only one who can solve your problems in life; others can guide you, but you have to do the work.

Meditation makes me a better person. It lights a candle in my darkest moments. I now manage my children a lot more effectively, I am a better listener, I connect with my husband on a deeper spiritual level, and I make better life decisions. Meditation taught me to get out of my own way and to operate out of love and compassion. It forces me to shut out the noise and simply listen to my inner voice, which guides me through life and tells me what to do and when to do it. The rest I leave up to God.

*Meditation empties all the garbage out; it cleanses your inside to make room for all the good things.*

### Creating Your Very Own Sanctuary at Home

Traditionally, it is best to meditate either first thing in the morning or last thing at night and stick with the same schedule every day. As a busy woman and/or mother this is sometimes impossible, so taking your escapes whenever you can is certainly ok.

Your meditation environment should be as clean and uncluttered as possible, even if it is a small space. An unencumbered space creates a more open feel and allows the positive energy that you create to flow through you and circulate freely. It also allows the negative energy you release to escape your environment.

An uncluttered environment also removes visual distractions that can intrude into your practice. Although your eyes will be closed, the last things they see while open can certainly shape your session. A Zen visual environment will send the appropriate cues to your brain that it, too, can be clutter-free. Free from noise, stress, and thoughts.

When you meditate it is best to wear loose, light colored clothing made of natural fibres. Wearing white allows your aura to radiate around your body, while wearing a bright color that resonates with a particular chakra will help balance and clear the energy in that part of your body. Always keep a wrap or light blanket to drape around your shoulders if you get cool.

The lighting in the environment should be soft and dim, preferably enhanced with candlelight. Burn sage to clear negative energy, and then light your favorite incense or aromatherapy oils. When you really start to fall in love with meditation, invest in a small wooden altar or Chinese stool and adorn it with whatever your heart desires. I have a Buddha statue, a Tibetan bell, nag champa incense, and a candle on my altar.

## Shavasana

Up until a few years ago, the closest I got to meditation was in Yoga when I would lie down at the end of a class for 5-15 minutes in Shavasana. I always loved this asana (pose) because you can really feel the energy moving through your body as it goes into a state of sensory withdrawal.

Quieting the mind and focusing on the breath while lying down in Shavasana (shah-VAH-sah-nah) (corpse pose) is a great place to start on your journey to meditation. It is a less intimidating position and a simple way to start training your mind to really stop. This pose makes it easier to be aware of the breath and of your state of mind.

If you already practice Yoga try to extend your time in Shavasana at a class. When things are really quiet at home, either later in the evening or early in the morning, put your Yoga mat down in your meditation area. Just lay on your back in the pose and let your body relax. Extend your time in this pose up to 20 or 30 minutes, if you can.

## Seated Meditation

Always meditate in the same place, on the floor with your legs crossed or in a half lotus position. It's best to use a meditation pillow or a thick, folded blanket to prop you upright and keep your spine straight. This will help you keep your knees lower than your hips, which is the proper position in this meditation posture.

Keep your shoulders rolled down and back, away from the ears, with your chest expanded comfortably. Lengthen your neck; tuck your chin slightly while keeping your gaze straight ahead. Your forehead should be at a 90-degree angle to the floor. All of this positioning is designed to create a long and straight spine, free from tension that could distract your practice.

## Guided Meditation

Another technique to really help you along is using a guided meditation. There are so many good ones, and everyone is drawn to different methods, so you should experiment and find the ones that resonate with you most. There is also an array of smart phone apps with meditation bells you can play that will ring out to signal the beginning and end of your session.

Meditation will change your life. It is an essential in your OM Formula, an ingredient you cannot live with out. If you start living and breathing from the inside, your life will magically fall into place. You will journey to places you could never have imagined and find peace, happiness, and love in abundance. You will never look back. Creating your own meditation sanctuary in your life every day for you to escape from the outside world, will give you that breathing space you need in your life to nourish your spirit.

*Be Still. Inhale. Exhale. Be Still.*

# *Gratitude*

**Gratitude is not only the greatest of all virtues, but also the leader
to all others. When you are grateful every other virtue
automatically appears in your life.**

Gratitude is one of the most powerful emotions we can embody and embrace. When you focus on being thankful, believe in the power of true appreciation, and radiate gratitude from you core, you will always live in abundance. Your positive outlook will draw more good things into your life: Love, Health, Wealth, Happiness, and so on.

One thing I know for certain is that if you work on being Grateful—I mean truly thanking God and thanking life every day for your blessings, letting your gratitude shine out from your heart—the rest seems to take care of itself. Life is easier and more abundant when you are grateful.

**"Happiness is not having what you want,
but wanting what you have."**

- Rabbi H. Schachtel

## DAILY MANTRA

### "I am Grateful For"

Your day should start and end with a simple mantra:

"I am grateful for . . ."

and then say everything that you are truly grateful for.

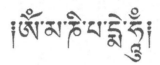

Mantra and meditation is a powerful way to start and/or end the day. Silencing the mind and opening our spirits to thank God and the Universe for our blessings seals in our intentions. When we program ourselves with gratitude, we live with a perspective of abundance and attract more good things into our lives. Be thankful and never take for granted the simplest things in life—a roof over your head, food on the table, good health, and all of the other riches, both great and small, that you have been blessed with.

There are a several things I thank God for everyday without needing to ponder. My children's health and safety is first. Second is the health of my husband, family, friends, and loved ones. Third comes my own health, heart, and blessings. Our family thanks God whenever we sit down to eat. My husband and I teach our kids that food is something to be extremely grateful for; millions of people go without basic necessities like food and water every day.

### And This Too Shall Pass

Gratitude does not prevent difficult situations in life. Be grateful for the strength you have to face them, and move on from those difficulties once you have learned the lesson brought before you. Gratitude and the awareness that all situations will pass give you the ability to solve problems rationally and logically.

Understanding that bad situations are temporary allows us to always keep an eye on the light at the end of the tunnel and not get lost in the dark. On the flip side, remember that good situations are also temporary; such awareness naturally leads to savoring good moments and appreciating time spent with our loved ones.

Once you let the power of gratitude take over your being—once it's infused into every waking minute of your life, flowing in and out of your mind and body as often as your breath—you will forever change your life. Acknowledge your Creator for His blessings upon you, no matter how big or small they may be. When gratitude takes over, your aura will glow every color of the chakra spectrum. You will radiate light, and you will become a calming and uplifting presence to others around you, without them even knowing what's happening. Nothing need be said; the power of your true being will unfold.

Grateful people are by nature very optimistic, humble, caring, kind, and considerate. When you are truly grateful, you will live a more grounded, more spiritual, happier life. Be grateful for everything, and you will automatically attract what you truly need in life; where there were once only walls, magical doors will appear and start to open.

# Giving

"Give, and it will be given to you. Good measure, pressed down, shaken together, running over, will be put into your lap. For with the measure you use it will be measured back to you."

- Luke 6:38

The act of giving to someone without ever expecting anything in return is one of the most compelling ways to elevate your heart's vibrational energy. There is no greater joy in the world; it is love manifested as action.

Buddha taught that the act of giving carves out and prepares the Soul's garden bed to sow the seeds of spiritual growth. The value of giving is not determined by Earthly measures. It is the most fundamental of human virtues, and it gauges the depth of one's humanity and spiritual enlightenment.

Never underestimate the power of giving—the smallest act of giving can change somebody's life. When you give to another human being, altering the course of that person's life for the better, your actions create a ripple effect across the entire Universe.

Even if you don't have a lot of money to give away, there are so many other gifts that each of us have to share with others, be they hugs, smiles, kindness, love, or time. Giving somebody your time is one the most beautiful and meaningful things you can offer.

Giving undivided time and attention to your children is all they need to feel loved and valued. When my three-year-old son says to me, "Mommy get off your computer and play with me", I drop everything to sit with him and give him my time. I know that taking the time to call my family and friends just to talk and ask them how they are means a lot to them.

Giving not only helps the recipient but also makes you feel better deep inside, and your heart chakra blossoms. If you feel down, just go out and give something to someone. I guarantee it will lift your mood in an instant.

## Giving from the Heart

When you live in a big city, in your everyday travels you can pass at least 20 homeless people living and begging on the streets. If you are out and about quite a bit, like me, you see many more.

It is heart breaking to see that people's lives get to the point where they have nowhere to go and no food to eat. I give as much as I can when I instinctively feel that the money will go toward food and necessities, rather than enabling drug or alcohol dependency.

My 7-year-old daughter and I decided that as often as we can, we would put together grocery bags with enough healthy food and bottled water to feed a homeless person for a few days. We drive around and do this during the day, always making sure we stop to deliver it somewhere relatively safe. On top of the grocery bag we put an envelope in the bag with $5 in it and a message on the front that reads:

**"Someone somewhere needs your talent and special skills. Believe in yourself and you can change your life."**

I don't think that there is any greater joy than seeing the gratitude in a person's face when they get the grocery bag on the street and read the note. My only hope is that this simple act of kindness and the message they need to hear will crack the shell on them to let the light in, believing enough in themselves and opening to the possibility of miracles. Sometimes keeping hope alive is all we need to fortify and lift ourselves up.

I want my kids growing up knowing the value of simple things, never, ever taking for granted the blessed and loving life they have. There is no other way to teach your kids this lesson than through the experience of giving from the heart without expecting repayment.

## *Give to a Child in Need*

For every Om for the Mom book sold, a percentage of profit will go to two organizations I believe in.

**Friends of the Orphans -** This wonderful non-profit builds homes to raise and educate orphaned children, giving them a brighter future.

**www.friendsoftheorphans.org**

*Amani Kids* -  For over 10 years, Amani Children's Home has been dedicated to the protection of Tanzania's most vulnerable population: street children. Amani, which means "peace" in Swahili, was founded by Tanzanians, and over the course of the past decade has rescued hundreds of children from the perils of life on the streets, where they face numerous dangers including malnutrition and abuse. Amani provides healthy food, education, counseling and medical care for every street child who turns to us for help. When possible, children are reunified with (extended) families.

**www.amanikids.org**

I plan on taking my children to an orphanage in the near future to help them understand how lucky and privileged they are. However you can teach your children to give, do so. This is so important, not just for them, but for the greater good of the entire planet of less fortunate children around the world.

**"It's not how much we give but how much love we put into giving."**

- Mother Teresa

"Young people, who belong to the 21st century, have the opportunity to create a more peaceful world."

- Dalai Lama XIV

# *Prayer*

**"For me, prayer is a surge of the heart: it is a cry of recognition
and love embracing both trial and joy."**

-St. Therese of Lisieux

We all yearn for a connection to the spirit, even if we do not realize it. In a world crying out for God, I believe we have reached a new age—more people are shifting to finally find their tie to the Divine. Whatever your religion, faith, or belief system, the universal connection to God is to get down on your hands and knees on the Earth, humble and exalt yourself, and pray. I pray when I meditate, which is just another form of connecting to the Divine, but prayer can come in so many forms. There is no right or wrong, with prayer it just *is*.

### *Prayer is a Conversation with God*

God wants to have an intimate relationship with you; to experience this you have to be still. For some people prayer is in a temple, a mosque, or a church. For others, it is meditation. If you are open and willing, God will talk to you and give you the answers. We hear them in that small inner voice or the thought that does not come from our mind. The instinctive gut feeling that points the way, our inner guidance system—that's the voice of God.

*When you look at this world in all its glory, look with your heart, not your eyes, and you will start to see things you have never seen before.*

There are over 6 billion people living on this Earth. If you asked each and every one of them what they thought God looked like, you would get over 6 billion different answers. If God were to appear on this Earth, how would he appear so that each and every one of us could recognize Him (or Her)? How would we know it was really God?

If He appeared to you and you described Him to me, I would most likely say, "Well that's not how I pictured Him to be, I'm not sure that's God." Now, if you ask the majority of people who believe in God what he "feels like," imagining him through your heart and Soul rather than your eyes, most would say, "He feels like love."

*Love is the universal language that breaks all barriers and crosses all cultures and religions. Operate only out of love, and you will control your life, with God as your guide.*

When you close your eyes to go within, you tap into your inner being, whose clarity and scope of vision is more powerful than you can imagine. This is you connecting to the Divine. Do this on a regular basis, and you will begin to align yourself with the universal language and guidance system that God gave you to navigate through life.

*Look for signs, nothing is an accident or a coincidence, it is serendipity and God at work. Open your eyes, believe, and listen with your heart.*

I know that my godmother, Cath, and my Nana are with me at all times, as are my spiritual guides, angels, and God. I don't see them, but I feel them. I just know they are with me. They show me signs here on Earth every day. White feathers, a penny and a dime, the number 406, and the tingling on my neck and head are some of the things I see and experience every day. These are my signs and guides; part of your personal spiritual formula is to find your own and ask your loved ones to give these signs to guide you on your way.

When hard times present themselves, the first question you need to ask yourself is, "What is this teaching me?" I believe that God does not make mistakes and that He only presents us with difficult experiences for two reasons: either to teach us or help us grow, or to balance out our karma.

So whenever you can, pray with your heart, listen with your heart, and put your heart into learning God's lessons. You will never be led astray.

"Follow the shining ones, the wise, the awakened, the loving, for they know how to forbear. Whoever follows those who follow the way discovers his family, and is filled with joy. Follow them, as the moon follows the path of the stars. Look within. Be still. Free from fear and attachment, know the sweet joy of the way."

-Buddha

# *Forgiveness*

**"Forgiveness is the fragrance that the violet sheds on the heel that has crushed it. "**

-Mark Twain

Several years ago my sister and I were driving on a highway for a short day trip up to Noosa in Queensland, Australia. Less than two hours north of Brisbane when traffic is good, Noosa is in an area known as the Sunshine Coast, which is one of my favorite places in the world. The whole region has a very calming and spiritual energy.

On this particular day the sun was shining as we cruised north, and we took in the beauty of our surroundings, enjoying the journey as we looked forward to our destination. Engaged in a deep discussion about certain heart-wrenching and difficult circumstances within our family, we both savored the fresh air and fresh perspective that the beautiful drive brought.

At one point we began talking about how useless anger and resentment are, how they fail to achieve any good and actually cause a lot of damage. We both wished desperately for our loved ones to release the resentment that we felt was poisoning our whole family and to allow forgiveness to unburden their Souls.

After a few minutes, we came upon a white hippie van driving in the slow lane. The following words were painted there on the back of the van:

**"Holding on to anger and resentment is like drinking poison and waiting for the other person to die."**

- Buddha

Our mouths dropped, and we laughed. I could hardly believe it. I knew it was our spirit guides showing us that we were on the right path. We had witnessed firsthand the damage that unresolved blame and anger can cause over time; our guides were reminding us the value of learning from the mistakes of others.

That day our Souls fully absorbed the meaning of those words.

We all have been hurt in our lifetime by the unkind or thoughtless words and actions of other people, which often leave us feeling, angry, offended, bitter, and even vengeful. The ego loves to hold onto these debilitating emotions, which serve no purpose to our authentic spiritual self.

Forgetting something and forgiving something are two different things. Forgiveness releases you from the past, the burden and the pain, and truly sets you free. As long as you harbor bitter resentment and burning anger, no matter how deeply buried, you can never heal and move on. Instead, you are left with a scorched spirit. You and the people you love are the ones who are affected when you let these feelings take control of your life.

The decision to forgive someone is one of the hardest things to do, but when you finally turn that light on and let go, you make room in your heart for gratitude, happiness, and love. When you choose not to give any power to a hurtful experience that someone else has induced, you take control of your own destiny and your spiritual well-being.

**"The weak can never forgive.**
**Forgiveness is the attribute of the strong."**

- Gandhi

The healing power of forgiveness is an essential ingredient in your formula for spiritual growth. You must forgive everyone who has done you wrong and harm, and always forgive yourself for your mistakes and transgressions.

**"You will not be punished for your anger; you will be punished by your anger."**

- Buddha

# *Soul Cleansing*

"And the smoke of the incense, which came with the prayers of the saints, ascended up before God out of the angel's hand."

- Revelations 8:4

*The simple act of cupping water in your hands to nourish and cleanse the body. Burning incense and sage to cleanse the air. For it is the water we drink and air that we breathe that keeps us alive.*

*These are simple daily practises that nourish your body and Soul.*

## Incense

Whether it is in a Hindu temple, a Buddhist monastery, or your very own home, incense uplifts the mood and causes a powerful spiritual alteration. The subtle power of these mystical fragrances creates a calming aromatic ambiance that dramatically shifts your energy to balance and harmonize the mind, body, and spirit. Burning incense sticks helps to remove negative energy in the environment and rejuvenates the mind.

I cannot say enough about the power of incense and its healing properties. Since the beginning of civilization, temples and monasteries have fiercely guarded their own secret formulas for incense.

What your mind and body need dictates the scents that you are drawn to; so always choose a fragrance that has a pleasing and peaceful effect on your spirit. I particularly love Nag Champa—its sandalwood base is very grounding and centering. I burn it every day at my desk, in my bathroom, and throughout our living environment, and a box goes with me every time I travel.

### "Smudging" With Sage

Burning sage—also known as "smudging your environment"— is a powerful way to clear blockages and remove negative energy. Any time you smudge your environment, make it a ritual. Cleanse yourself with the sage first, and ask the Divine to help clear away any trapped energy within yourself and your environment that no longer serves you. Make sure that the smoke gets into every corner, and pay special attention to areas of your space that feel "heavy" or "dark."

## *Water Cleansing*

Water nourishes, gives life, cleanses the body, and purifies the spirit. I love water—its pure scent, the way it sparkles in the sunlight, and how it feels as it washes over the skin and how it purifies your body when you drink it. Water cleansing rituals are among the most sacred and calming techniques for bodily and spiritual renewal, and they play an important role in many religious traditions.

Christians use water for baptisms and for blessings as they enter and leave a church. Muslims cleanse themselves with water before each of their five daily prayers, a practice known as Wudu. In Jewish traditions, immersion in a gathering of water, known as the Mikveh, is required before conversion, marriage, or the Sabbath. Hindus also cleanse themselves with water before praying—their temples have dedicated areas for bathing hands and feet.

My dream is to install a Japanese bamboo foot washing station in my bathroom so I can cleanse my feet before I go to bed every night, instead of bathing them in the sink.

**"Take a music bath once or twice a week for a few seasons. You will find it is to the Soul what a water bath is to the body."**

- Oliver Wendell Holmes

One of the best sanctuary escapes in your own home is a steamy, oil and mineral infused bath soak. I set up my bathroom at home just as I would have done for a client when I owned my wellness spa retreat.

The following is my personal formula for the perfect bathtub Soul sanctuary:

> ~ Dim the lights or turn them off, light candles, put on your favorite relaxation music, and lock the door.

> ~ Pour 1-3 cups of magnesium minerals in the water to help relax muscles and reduce stress and anxiety. Magnesium chloride minerals are the best. They absorb through your

skin at a cellular level to help you unwind. Like drinking vitamins through your skin! Epsom salts (magnesium sulphate) can also be effective.

~ Add a few drops of aromatherapy oil for fragrance and to really help you escape. My favorite is Ylang Ylang, but you may also want to experiment and find the best essential for you. Like incense, pick the aromatherapy oils the smell best to you; your body will be attracted to what it needs. You can also choose your oils based on specific, targeted effects that you hope to achieve: relaxation, calming, centering and revitalisation.

~ A bath with a (small) glass of wine or a warm cup of tea will soothe anyone's senses in a few minutes

~ Allow yourself at least 20 minutes to soak in the tub, but stay as long as you'd like.

I also find refuge in the shower. Sometimes I even meditate in the shower if I have had a really stressful day. I turn off the lights, light candles, turn on my music, and sit in lotus pose directly under the water so that it falls directly on the top of my head. This practice soothes my mind and washes any tension away in minutes. It is also wonderful for opening the crown chakra located at the top of your head. The crown chakra is violet in color and known as the thousand-petal Lotus flower. It is the opening to our higher power, creativity, and inspiration from the divine.

Water cleanses and hydrates us—it is the essence and nourishment of all life. When we connect with water it embraces us fully, leaving no part untouched.

Never take water for granted because one billion people around the world lack a safe daily supply of water for drinking and bathing. Be grateful for the clean water you have every day, you are truly blessed.

# *Music & Dance*

**"Music is what feelings sound like."**

- Unknown

Music is the voice of feelings, the melody of the heart's song, and the poetry of the Soul. For me there is nothing quite like music to make you smile and bring the sun out to shine light in the darkest corners of your life. The restorative, healing benefits of music cannot be put into words. Something about the combination of a tune and lyrics has an indescribable effect on our well-being.

**"When you are in love you hear the melody and the tune of a song, when you are sad and alone you hear the words."**

- Unknown

I love so much music; I could never narrow it down enough to tell you my favorite artists. It really depends upon my mood. I love Jazz on Sunday mornings at home, Funk and Disco when I am out dancing, Classical and Opera when I am painting and creating art, Rock n Roll when I want to sing out loud in my car, and Flamenco guitars and Latin when I am dancing with my husband (he is an unbelievable dancer).

Spiritual and Zen music is what I listen to most because it connects with who I am as a person. I listen to it during Yoga, and meditation, for stress relief, and when I am writing. It's the melody and the movement that guides me along my path and holds my hand on my journey. It inspires me and opens up my Soul to allow the words to freely come out.

*Wherever I am I usually have my music playing, my Nag Champa incense burning, and a hot tea next to me.*

**"Music is the wine, which inspires one to new generative processes, and I am Bacchus who presses out this glorious wine for mankind and makes them spiritually drunken."**

- Ludwig Van Beethoven

## *Sing Every Day*

One of the reasons I so love Kundalini Yoga is that we chant and sing in the practice.

**"When you chant OM, let it vibrate on the solar plexus. All the power of creation, the whole Universe is present deep inside you. Let it vibrate in each cell of your body."**

- Swami Vishwananda

However you connect to the spirit, either through chanting or singing, I highly recommend letting it resonate with your energy every day in some form. If you are shy and love to sing, find a private place where you can sing with abandon and not worry about other people hearing. I love to sing in the shower and in the car. Just let it out!

## *Dance Every Day*

Unless you are a professional dancer, chances are you don't dance every day of your life. If you do, good for you! Dance is the freest form of physical expression. When a song or rhythm resonates with your spirit, acknowledging that resonance through movement is the natural reaction. Squashing the urge to move can lead to energy blockages. I love to dance with my girlfriends, and I love dancing with my husband. He can dance everything from; Salsa to Disco. I turn up the music and dance with my kids all the time; we bust out dance parties on a regular basis and just let loose and get silly.

Keep your energy flowing freely and dance like nobody's watching. This will also keep you young at heart throughout your life.

# *Tea*

**"Tea is nought but this: First you heat the water, then you make the tea. Then you drink it properly. That is all you need to know."**

- Sen Rikyu, 16th Century Tea Master

The simple act of drinking tea is similar to the practice of Zen meditation. Drinking tea or a hot cup of coffee and savoring each sip helps us reflect, quiet our minds, and tune in to the present moment. Hundreds of years ago the Samurai warriors longed for their quiet times drinking tea—it was an escape from the turmoil they were living in. Today is not so different: our busy, hectic lives need times of peace and refuge. The simple practice of sitting and drinking tea can sometimes be all we need to enhance our lives and still our minds.

Traditional Japanese tea ceremonies elevate the experience to an art form—tea service is performed meticulously and never rushed. The ritual is designed to make you focus on the simplicity and pleasure that is right in front of you.

Like meditation, your own personal tea ceremony can quiet your mind and fill you with the power of being in the now. In addition to the psychic benefits associated with tea rituals, there are also many health benefits associated with tea that are now recognized all over the world. Green tea can assist in weight loss, protect the immune system, and perhaps slow down the aging process with its powerful antioxidants.

Many times throughout the day I sit down, stop everything, get off my computer, abandon my phone, and quietly sit and sip on a cup of tea or espresso. The first thing I do in the morning to start my day is have my espresso and the last thing I do before I go to bed at night is drink my tea.

My Nana gave me a beautiful 100-year-old tea set that sat in her china cabinet for 60 years, never once used for drinking tea, but did a great job of collecting dust. She would come to my house for a visit every week when I lived near her, and I would serve her tea in the China set. At first she was scared to drink from it, lest it break. I said to her, "This tea set is special, used for special moments. Those special moments are every day of your life, and I can't think of a better occasion than sitting here with you now. Now let's enjoy drinking from this beautiful, 100-year- old China set, shall we?"

So, if you have a tea set sitting around collecting dust, take it out and use it to savor in one of life's simple meditative art forms and pleasures.

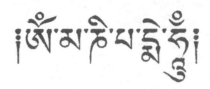

"In my own hands I hold a bowl of tea; I see all of nature represented in its green color. Closing my eyes, I find green mountains and pure water within my own heart. Silently sitting alone and drinking tea, I feel these become part of me.

What is the most wonderful thing for people like myself who follow the Way of Tea?

My answer: the oneness of host and guest created through 'meeting heart to heart' and sharing a bowl of tea."

- The Fifteenth Urasenke Grand Tea Master, Soshitsu Sen

# Life's Simple Moments

**"It is always the simple that produces the marvelous."**

- Amelia Barr

My Great Aunt, who was also given the blessing of being my Godmother, passed away a little over six years ago, the day after my daughter's first birthday. She was a living, breathing angel on this Earth and as sweet, pure, and loving as anyone I have ever met. She embodied angelic grace with everything that she did.

She loved to sing at church, and she made sure that everyone heard that songbird of a voice she had. Her favorite song was "Tiptoe Through the Tulips," and every time we paid her a visit she would be singing it as we skipped up her front path.

Her home was my refuge. She lived humbly, and there was a comfort and peace in her home like I have never experienced anywhere else—I always felt my heart was at rest there.

One of my favorite memories growing up was the giant macadamia nut tree in the back of her yard. There were deep, cracked crevices and holes all over the cement path next to the tree, 20 years worth of memories from the whole family cracking those nuts open with giant bricks. She would sit out on the back porch and watch us as she ate her favorite ice cream, "Have A Heart", a chocolate-coated vanilla ice cream shaped into the most perfect love heart. It was very fitting and no coincidence, as she had the biggest heart of anyone I knew, and she loved me unconditionally. Whenever I was with her, I felt safe and at home.

*As I write this section my head is tingling, a sign that she is here caressing my head as she always did when she was here on this Earth.*

Remember the simple things in life because one day you will look back on these moments and realize they were the big things.

## Life's Simple Moments

ཨྃ་མ་ཎི་པ་དྨེ་ཧྃ།

- Making tea, smelling the aroma, and sipping it while going into a meditative and quiet place inside.

- Smelling your flowers. Getting out in the garden; enjoying the act of watering a plant, nourishing it and giving it life.

- Taking a bath, feeling the water wash over your skin— really feeling it.

- Hanging some wind chimes near a door or window, sitting quietly and listening to the sweet sounds in the wind.

- Sitting quietly on the floor in your sanctuary space. Going within and meditating as long as you can. Journeying to the inside of you.

- Hugging, kissing, and loving your family and friends every day.

- Bathing in the vibrational sounds of a Gong bath after meditating.

- Sitting on a park bench, observing the trees, breathing the fresh air.

- A picnic on the beach or in a park.

- Smelling the rain after a shower, and then looking for the rainbow.

- Watching the sunrise and the sunset.

- Sitting under a full moon and harvesting its energy.

- Watching your kids run and play in the park.

- Smiling and feeling the smile on the inside.

- Swimming in the ocean and floating.

- Yoga stretching for 5 minutes just because.

- Eating ice cream with your kids on a hot summer day.

- Dancing with a loved one at home with all the lights out and just a candle burning.

- Singing in the shower or in the car.

- Taking your shoes off and feeling the Earth, sand, and grass on your feet.

- Sleeping on fresh, clean sheets.

- Listening to your favorite music.

- Meditating on incense, watching the smoke dance around the room.

- Walking a labyrinth and meditating.

- Staring at your children while they are peacefully asleep.

- Tickling and blowing bubbles with your children.

- Sitting by a fireplace with a glass of wine.

- Watching snowflakes fall.

- Laughing till you cry.

- Crying to cleanse the Soul and wash away worry.

- Painting, creating, writing poetry, playing music ~ anything creative.

**"Enjoy the little things in life, for one day you will look back and realize they were the big things."**

- Robert Brault

Create your own favorite simple moments in your journal. Copy this and put the list on your fridge, your vision board or anywhere you can see this daily, to remind you of what's really important.

*Journey Your World*

**"Though we travel the world over to find the beautiful, we must carry it with us or we find it not."**

- Ralph Waldo Emerson

Travel, for me, is the essence if life. Experiencing new places, meeting new cultures, and embracing new traditions opens your mind and Soul. When it comes to seeing and appreciating the wondrous extent of God's creations, there is no food more nourishing to the Soul than travel.

I have been so blessed and fortunate in my life to travel and live in many different parts of this beautiful world—Australia, China, Indonesia, Thailand, Dubai, Kuwait, Fiji, India, England, France, Belgium, Germany, Italy, Spain, The Caribbean, and Mexico to name a few. I have immersed myself in other cultures, eating their foods, walking their corner of the Earth, learning their history, living in their homes, and praying according to their religious traditions.

The most valuable lesson I have learned from all of my worldly travels is that the languages we speak, the colors of our skin, the religions we embrace, and the traditions we live by separate us only in the physical sense. In the spiritual sense, we are all one. We are all connected to the One source, to the beauty of God. We are all part of the same beautiful canvas he has painted for us.

The true beginning of my journey to myself began when I left home at the age of fifteen, moving from Australia to the USA without my family. I had no fear, and I knew that without a doubt that my spirit and God guided me along the way. I have always felt like a travelling gypsy, fluttering from one place to another and yearning to journey every inch of the globe that I possibly could. Every one of my journeys has shaped my Soul and made me who I am today.

My travels to the Middle East taught me how peaceful these people are. I observed their complete dedication and devotion to God, demonstrated through prayer rituals that took place five times a day. Hearing the calls to prayer echoing through the city sent chills through my body. It is truly beautiful. Islam is a culture of love with a deep connection to God.

When I chanted in temples in Thailand with Buddhists, I felt a different kind of call echoing through my Soul. It felt so natural, as if I had done it every day, and I realized that I had been there in a previous life. I then understood my deeply rooted passion for Buddhist philosophy and everything it embodies.

I lived in Florence, Italy at the end of my fourth year of Art School. I love this country with every fiber of my being—the culture of passion, the food, the clothes, the people, the language, and the arts. When I lived there I savored every moment, wandering the meandering cobble stone streets and getting lost along the way. When the church bells rang throughout the towns, I would sit in the nearest piazza, close my eyes and allow the sound to vibrate through my spirit.

My professor there arranged for us to eat with the monks in Assisi and organized a private viewing of the Sistine chapel, where we all laid down on the floor and gazed for hours at the beauty of Michelangelo's masterpieces. These life experiences can never be taken from me.

I find it difficult to express the true impact of these and other experiences, the special place they hold in my Soul. Perhaps "lost for words" is the best description, and perhaps therein lies the true beauty. The real wonders of the world are tucked away in those moments hidden between breath and heartbeat, when we step outside ourselves to revel in an experience, moment-to-moment, utterly lost for words. I have been truly blessed.

The experience of travel is different for all of us. Travel is a luxury in life that I am beyond grateful for. Although travelling to other countries is a big part of my life, it may or may not be part of your journey. You can find life's hidden wonders just around the corner.

Travelling outside of your environment to take a drive in the country or to visit a new park or beach opens your eyes to new experiences. Watching foreign films, travel shows, and documentaries; eating at ethnic restaurants; listening to world music; dancing with other cultures; and connecting with people from other traditions right in your community—all of these things open your eyes and give you a taste of

138

what the world has to offer. Don't be afraid to leave the comforts of what you know. Step outside your usual surroundings and your comfort zone to step outside of yourself. I promise you that opening yourself to the world brings you closer to God. Explore all that He has created, all that makes this world so special and unique.

Life's real travel experience lies in savoring the journey. The destination is not as important. Moving consciously through the labyrinth of your life is what God wants from you. Staying open to all possibilities and accepting all people from every faith and culture is the essence of travel for me. It's part of my journey to my Soul.

Make your day-to-day life its own mystical experience. Look at every flower, sunrise, shell, tree, cloud, and bird with wonder. See the awe of creation inside your partner, your husband, your family, your beautiful children, and, most importantly, yourself. This is your journey, your travel experience to love and behold.

So take yourself away every day and look forward to the new possibilities God has to offer you. Always maintain that state of wonder and awe you had when you were a child. See with your heart, and you will look at life in a completely different way and travel to places from your wildest dreams.

### "It is better to travel well than to arrive."

- Buddha

# Soul Reflections

The intention of the first part of this book is to help light as many candles as possible in areas of darkness. The more people in this world who operate out of love, the more enlightened our society becomes.

This book is meant to be a tool to help guide you on your journey to find yourself. Do the work to become the best person you can possibly be for the sake of yourself, your family, friends, and children, and for the greater good of all. In order to crack your outer shell and access the light inside, you must engage consciously in your efforts every day for at least 40 days. After that time your work will still continue, but you'll find it much easier. It will eventually become a part of you.

The period of 40 days is very symbolic, and it has been used by God to represent a period of testing or judgment. Forty days is the length of time necessary to accomplish any major or radical changes in your life. Once you pass this threshold your spirit will adopt the practice as part of you. Moses and Jesus were both tested for 40 days of fasting in the desert, in order to accomplish a major part of God's plan.

To initiate a true and lasting transformation of self, here are my recommendations for things to incorporate as part of your life's personal spiritual formula:

~ Follow the mantras and meditations at the end of each section.

~ Repeat the quotes throughout this book that resonate with you—say them over and over, write them down, and place them throughout your environment wherever you'll see them every day.

~ Start practicing Yoga and Meditation, and work on only you.

~ Wear white or light colored clothes when you meditate and sleep, or wear a bright color that resonates with particular chakras that need work. If you cover or drape your head with a scarf while meditating, you seal in the meditative energy and more easily store the wisdom and clarity you gain through meditation.

~ Get outside in nature more.

~ Exercise and walk.

~ Start eating healthily to go on your own personal life retreat for 40 days. (Please consult your doctor if you have any health problems to make sure this change in eating will work for you.)

~ Eat a raw food diet if possible.

~ Limit or cut out sugar and red meat.

~ Avoid refined carbohydrates.

~ Eliminate processed/packaged foods.

~ Limit your dairy intake.

~ Get plenty of fiber – legumes are a great source of both fiber and protein.

~ Disconnect yourself from alcohol and replace it with lemon water.

~ Invest in a juicer and drink fresh vegetable juice daily.

~ Limit your time around negative and energy-draining people; if you can't avoid them, imagine yourself in a large glass egg that negative energy can't pass through.

~ Get rid of the attachments and the things that will not serve you.

~ Acquire only what you need in your life, don't go buy things to fill a void.

~ Practice the small rituals daily, the ones that resonate with you.

~Step outside of yourself, and open yourself to new perspectives every day.

~ Look for signs and miracles. Believe they are real and life will magically unveil all of its restorative power and beauty for you.

~ Remember to pay attention to all of the beauty that surrounds you and to the people you meet along the way, for it is the journey that matters. The destination is not as important.

~ If there are simple things that make you happy, do them and create your own formula and prescription for a happy, spiritual and holistic life.

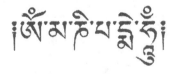

The more consistent and disciplined you are over the 40 days, the stronger you will become. Whenever you need to know what to do, quiet your mind, go inside of yourself and ask the question you want answers to.

I am giving you the basic principles to work on and the tools and techniques that have changed my life, but for you it may be different. Remember you have all the answers inside of you. Everything you need to know is within you, and you just have to quiet yourself down regularly to hear the voice.

This is your life, so you need to create a plan and formula that will fit your schedule and routine. My simple advice would be to create a 7-day plan and then repeat that religiously until you have reached your 40 days. Keep it simple and adjust accordingly.

Small and subtle shifts are the best ways to make change. Don't try to make too many radical changes in your life overnight, or you will feel overwhelmed and give up.

If, for example, your diet does not even closely resemble the list of foods I mentioned earlier, don't change everything at once. Introduce small changes here and there, and wait until they stick before making any other changes. Life is not a sprint, it's a marathon, and your goal is to make positive changes that will last a lifetime.

Remember the best way for you to predict your future is for you to create it. You are the producer, the author, the artist, and the musician of your own life. You are the storyteller, so write the best script for your life ahead.

Once you do the work on yourself and are happy with what you find, then your true, authentic self will begin to emerge—the one who operates out of love, gratitude, and compassion. All of your relationships with others, including your children, will become happier as a result of you taking care of your spiritual self first.

You are a woman capable of more things than you can possibly imagine. There is no limit to the possibilities in your life. You have to let go of fear, embrace the possibility of falling down, and never be afraid to try something that you believe in. Believe in yourself first and love yourself more than you do now because there is no one on this Earth that deserves your love more than you. Commit yourself to yourself, and I promise that your life will magically change.

**"I vow to let go of all worries and anxiety in order to be light and free..."**

- Thich Nhat Hanh

The tallest towers, the grandest temples, and the most beautiful trees withstand the most powerful storms because their foundations and roots are solidly in this Earth. Stand firmly, know who you are, and be proud of the person you are capable of being.

When you shine with the light of the Divine, you will take on this world as a peaceful warrior woman who embodies strength, nobility, grace, and gratitude. You will walk the labyrinth of this Earth steadily with one foot in front of the other, knowing that you are always moving forward in the peaceful, loving, and happy way that God intended you to live.

# Soul Meditation & Mantra

## "Finding Your Place in Spirituality"

### (Prepared By Karampal Kaur)

Tuning in and centering before a meditation:

{Chant Three Times}

**Ong namo guru dev namo**

"I bow to the infinite and the divine teacher within."

{Chant } Kirtan Kriya

**Sa Ta Na Ma**

Meditation (Chant for 18 minutes)

Feel comfortable with the flow of life and find your place in the Universe. It's easy to get lost in the labyrinth of life! Dwell in the notion that you belong to a continuous cycle of life- always learning, recreating, and evolving. This meditation will enhance your intuition, allow you to be guided by your spirit and will align you with the divine.

We will use the seed or in Yoga we call it the "bij" of the words Sat Nam meaning, *my divine true identity*. There are four principle components of this exercise: Mantra, Mudra, Voice and Visualization.

## 1. Chant SAA

Index finger touches the thumb- visualize infinity, the beginning, "the cosmos", feel expansive!

## 2. Chant TAA

Middle finger touches thumb- visualize life on Earth, existence, birth.

## 3. Chant NAA

Ring finger touches thumb- visualize death, change and the transformation of consciousness.

## 4. Chant MAA

Pinkie touches the thumb- visualize rebirth renewal, the joy of the infinite.

As you recite this mantra meditate on the inflow of cosmic energy coming through the crown and out of your brow point. In an "L" form beginning each sound at the top of your head (S) and end each sound as it comes through the brow (AA). This stimulates the pituitary and pineal glands, which enhance your intuition.

### *Let's Start.*

Sit straight in Easy pose (with your legs crossed) and meditate with your eyes closed to your third eye (located between your eyebrows in the center of your forehead.)

Begin to chant the Mantra **Sa Ta Na Ma** out loud for 3 minutes (don't forget your hand positions) and meditate on your awareness to all things in the world.

~ Then Whisper for 3 minutes - experiencing the longing to belong.

~ Meditate in silence- "mentally" vibrating the mantra for 6 minutes.

~ Back to whisper for 3 minutes

~ Back to chanting out loud for 3 minutes

**To End:** Inhale deeply and suspend your breath as long as comfortable and gently exhale and relax the breath. Sit in stillness and the peace you created for at least 1 minute

146

"In the end these things matter most. How well did you love? How fully did you live? How deeply did you let go?"

- Buddha

*Whatever words follow I AM in your life is what will come looking for you.*

(prepared by Vanessa)

ཨོཾ་མ་ཎི་པ་དྨེ་ཧཱུྃ།

Sit quietly at the beginning and at the end of everyday and chant this I AM Mantra to connect to your true authentic self ~ your spirit.

I AM PURE SPIRIT

I AM LOVING ENERGY

I AM FORGIVNESS

I AM GRATEFUL

I AM BREATH

I AM GIVING

I AM LOVE

I AM A SOUL


I AM GOD

# *Sutra 2*

## *The Divine Feminine*

***There is no greater divinity than the feminine spirit.***

*What is a woman? To me a woman is a symbol of infinity,
embracing divinity while radiating love, light, and purity.*

*A woman is more than the family she nurtures and
what she does day to day.*

*Woman is a powerful being, full of grace, love, strength, and
nobility.*

*Woman gives birth to man.*

The tools, teachings, and techniques to assist a woman in finding her true power have been around since the beginning of civilization. I recall a story about an ancient tribe that would stand at the base of a mountain while a woman draped in white ascended to the summit, raised her arms in the air in a V-shaped formation, and prayed to God. She was known as the connector— the spiritual adapter—between God and the Earth.

In Indian history the stories of mystical and magical Goddesses are endless. Sara Swati—the Goddess of learning, knowledge, the arts, music, magic, and eloquence—created the first alphabet, and many consider her the mother of all life.

Lakshmi was known as the Goddess of good fortune, wealth, prosperity, and beauty; she represented all things feminine. Durga, the warrior Goddess, was invincible in battle, and she was created by the Gods to destroy the monster that was threatening their power. Devi was the great mother Goddess responsible for Earth, fire, air and water.

In earlier times in certain Native American tribes, women owned their children first. The women owned the houses and not only held the political, spiritual, and medicinal power but also held power of autonomy and equality. Women were the backbone of the tribe.

In modern Western society, so much of what we learn about what it means to be a woman is simply external. In our hyper-commercialized world, we are constantly bombarded with very narrow, very externalized messages about what a woman is. But what about *who* a woman is? Where are those messages? They are out there and growing stronger every day, but there is still a whole lot of noise to overcome.

Every woman is capable of tapping into the universal power within her to begin manifesting her greatest dreams and desires. By first lying your foundation as a spiritual and holistic human being you gain access to your authentic self. This opens the door for you to understand the true nature of your feminine spirit.

A woman who truly understands the power and grace within her can achieve anything. Start building yourself up and take that first step on your journey to empowerment by understanding the true meaning of this mantra: I AM WOMAN.

*The feminine spirit is such a beautiful and magical essence. We all have this spirit but many have built up a hard shell around it to protect the spirit and shelter us from the world.*

*Women don't know how wonderful they are and just how much power they possess.*

*Women don't need to act like men to gain power.*

*They need to act like a graceful, elegant, strong woman to gain power ~ **this is how you rule your world.***

# The Gentle Warrior Spirit

Tibetan Buddhist legend says that the kingdom of Shambhala existed somewhere in the remote Himalayas many centuries ago. Some believe this is purely a myth, and some believe that it still exists today, hidden away. Still others believe the kingdom of Shambhala has always been a symbolic legend about a real place that can be found inside of us.

In this last interpretation, the Shambhala kingdom represents pure enlightenment without the guidance of religion. The foundations of this mystical kingdom of spirit are rooted in the collective human wisdom that can help solve the world's problems. This basic teaching embodies the peace and gentleness at the core of the Buddhist tradition.

Shambhala is also about accepting reality and the world you live in, being happy with what you have, and remaining steadfast and strong but flexible through the currents of life. Real happiness is born when you learn how to enjoy very simple experiences. This softens you, helping you radiate more compassion and love. With this approach to life you will go with the flow more, be less resistant to the tides of change, and find that things bother you less and less.

Your Yoga and Meditation practice can help you get to the place inside of you where Shambhala resides. When you spend more time in the present moment, breathe mindfully, listen intently, and observe the world around you with awe and wonder, you will then become excited and amazed at the power you can attract and hold within your spirit.

For most of my life, up until about 12 years ago when I experienced my first spiritual shift, I could not even sit down quietly to read a book, let alone have enough peace and discipline to write one.

Moments of quiet reflection would force me to think about my life too much. I would inevitably start thinking of everything I didn't like about it, and I would catch glimpses of what I didn't like about myself. I was better off tuning it out by always having noise, distractions, and activity around me.

I was also afraid to be alone; the feeling of abandonment would creep in, and I did not want to face my fear of that. I would even sleep with the TV on just to hear the noise and not have to observe the silence.

When I was nine years old a man with a stocking over his face broke into my family home at 2 am and attempted to either kidnap me or hurt me. This one horrible moment that happened to me as a child left me paralyzed with fear for most of my life. For almost 25 years after that, I slept with not only the TV on but also the lights on, and I never slept with my back facing the door.

I will never forget the details of that night as long as I will live. Our cat was on the end of my bed sleeping, and thank God my father was awake that night at 2 am to hear me scream. As I suffocated under the attacker's grip over my mouth, he lifted his hand to let me breathe for a second. I went into survival mode, and in that second I screamed so loudly it saved my life.

My father called out, "Are you Ok?" and within a split second the man was gone down the hallway and out the door. I immediately ran to my baby brothers' room where the three of them slept, gathered them all together, and brought them to our father's room to keep them safe from harm.

For the next two years I slept on the floor of my father's room every night on a bed I would make from comforters and blankets. I did not sleep in my room again until we moved to a new house. Even then, for as long as I can remember, I would make sure there was a dead bolt on my bedroom door in every house we lived in until I moved out of home.

I think this horrific moment in my life, coupled with the pain of my parents getting divorced earlier that same year, kept me in a perpetual state of fear and disconnection for too long. These two painful memories imprinted on me for many years. I never went to counselling—I just dealt with it myself, or at least I tried to.

To further complicate matters, I became the caretaker of my family and also took on the role of "fixer." I was the eldest of all six of my siblings—my nickname was "mother duck"—and for the next 30 years of my life I played the role of guiding, inspiring, and constantly mending the wounds of a broken family.

I'm not sure if amicable divorces actually exist, but our family's was not one of them. I don't think a family can ever be prepared for a divorce and the damage it does to everyone's lives, especially the children's for years to come. It takes a lot of work and adjustment to find your way again as a family.

While I may have appeared happy and bubbly to others, I walked around with a lot of fear deep down inside, harboring the role of a victim. I was subconsciously afraid of being abducted or abandoned, and both feelings played off each other whenever they could creep into my life.

For many years I was so disconnected from my true self that I had completely forgotten how difficult things were when my parents were still together. As far back as I could remember, my early childhood years were happy—almost perfect, even. When I began my spiritual journey and started living from the inside, that's when I began to remember all the terrible fighting between my parents from about the age of six.

To escape the madness, I would make a princess tent in the backyard of my house by draping a purple velvet blanket over a pole. I sat in there alone, sometimes all day, pretending that I was somewhere else in the world—somewhere where there was only love, peace, and happiness. I took my dolls and tea set in there, and I would tell them happy stories and my dreams of travelling to far off lands.

What I did not know at the time was that at 15 years old I would leave home to move overseas without my family to go build my dreams and find peace and happiness. So I always say, "Be careful what you wish for." In a lot of ways the move for me was good, as I was no longer in the middle of a family war that became too much for me to bear any longer. I could not be happy anymore for people that did not want to find happiness in themselves.

I knew this in my heart then, but it took me another 23 years to fully learn that lesson and truly let it go. I kept running for far too long from the things that I did not want to face inside of me. I did not want to deal with my fears of being alone and of not being loved, so I was always in a relationship whether it was good or bad. I worked, I went to school, and I moved around in my twenties like a butterfly with a jet engine on my back.

That scared and fearful person inside of me has moved on. It took some time to heal from my childhood pain, but I did. I dedicated myself to doing the work, and it paid off. Whereas I was once scared to be alone, I now savor those moments in complete silence. I love being able to sit and have no distractions, no books, no music, and no noise. I love sitting there, just being. It's hard to believe that I ever lived my life happy but disconnected from the Source.

When you quiet your mind down it forces you to look at yourself for who you really are—the good and the not so good. A lot of us don't like what we see, and to avoid dealing with it we keep busy, keep moving, and don't ever stop. Whatever it is that's inside you that you'd rather not see, ignoring it does not make it go away and does not stop it from affecting your life.

Whatever stuff you're holding onto will never go away until it has taught you what you need to know. Learn the lesson, good or bad, let it go like a message bottle out to sea, and start new. When you start looking at your truth, don't judge yourself. If you don't like what you see, do the work and change it.

*Every second of your life, with every breath you take, you have a new chance to make a conscious change in your life. With every breath you get a second chance to choose the path of your journey.*

None of us are perfect, but when you accept yourself for all that you are and own that, you can start to do the work on yourself. Whatever you are harboring, it is no different than if you are a drug addict or an alcoholic. Until you can accept who you are, you will never be able to do the work to change. You don't have to go shout it from the rooftops or wear a scarlet letter; you just have to answer to yourself.

**"I am not what happened to me.**

**I am what I choose to become."**

- Carl Yung

## *Face and Embrace Your True Self to Become a Shambhala Warrior Woman*

To get through this life, you need not toughen up and build a shell around your spirit. You can become strong at your core and use that power to become a graceful warrior. A Shambhala warrior woman is soft and gentle but takes on the world with strength. She becomes resilient to life. When trouble arises or conflict rears its disruptive head, she practices keeping her feet firmly on the ground with her head held up high. She stays connected at her core, just like in Yoga, and she will find she can withstand any kind of weather. Whether that conflict is with her partner, her children, a family member, or a co-worker, or one of many life's challenges, she will be able to handle the situation more successfully.

Keep calm and breathe like in your meditation practice, and you will be able to navigate the situation into calmer waters. The Kundalini breath of fire technique works wonders at these times.

When you apply these ancient strategies for modern challenges in day-to-day life, you will be able to take on whatever life throws at you—one breath and one graceful step at a time.

# The Jewel in the Lotus

The Jewel in the Lotus is a Buddhist mantra of compassion. The jewel refers to your consciousness, and the lotus represents the heart that is the source of love and energy.

The lotus flower is one of the most intriguing, sensual, magical, and beautiful of all flowers; every morning it emerges from muddy waters and blooms, unfolding each of its countless petals slowly to greet the warmth and energy of the sun.

I have always been drawn to lotus flowers, not only because of their beauty, but also because they symbolize rebirth and purity. During the night the lotus closes its petals and sinks back into the muddy water, only to emerge again under the sunlight of a brand new day.

The stem of the lotus is flexible, but it does not break. Traditional stories say the thicker and muddier the water the more exquisite the lotus is when it rises. If we can aim to flow like the Lotus Flower does through muddy waters, we can use nutrients from the muck to emerge more beautiful than ever before.

I like to visualize Lotus flowers all the time to quiet my mind in meditation. In order for something to work in your life you must practice it daily. It must become part of your life—how you drink water, eat food, bathe, walk—it needs to become part of who you are. Everything you do needs to be embedded in your Soul.

Become the lotus flower in all that you do, and you will radiate sensual, mysterious beauty as a flexible yet resilient woman.

# *Intuition*

**"Intuition is a spiritual faculty and does not explain,
but simply points the way."**

- Florence Scovel Shinn

We all possess intuition. It is that voice inside of us that does not need to be governed by our analytical brain. It keeps our lives on track, guides us on the paths we were meant to walk, and leads us to what we are destined to do. Learn to trust the feeling of intuition like it's your best friend.

None of us are born with a navigation book in our hands to guide us through life, but we are born with an inner GPS system to help point us in the right direction. When we ignore our inner GPS we make bad decisions.

Albert Einstein said that the intuitive mind is a sacred gift and the rational mind is a faithful servant. We live in a society that honors the servant, but you can do better than that. Listen on the inside. You are an intuitive being.

When we listen to the inner voice and learn how to really hear it, the paths that we get lost on get fewer and farther between. This is how we learn to navigate our way through the world and live the life we are meant to—this is how we evolve our Souls.

When you start looking at the world through the eyes of your heart, then you understand that your body is just a vessel that carries and protects your ethereal spirit. When we lead with our internal being, the spirit and Soul guide us, not the ego. Look with your heart to see the true meaning of any situation and make more sound judgments and decisions in your life.

All answers are within us already, but to hear them you have to pause and really listen. When you find breathing space and quiet your mind, your inner voice and intuition speaks loudly and clearly, and the ego's voice diminishes and shuts down.

When you become spiritually grounded you create a space where the ego cannot speak nor live, and the only way you make decisions is with your heart. Following your heart's desire will not make you a sappy pushover; as long as you couple it with warrior strength, you will step forward soundly and gracefully.

**When your mind and body are perfectly aligned and in sync you walk a path of pure enlightenment.**

## *Strengthening Your Intuition*

Over the years I have become very sensitive to other people's energy. I can now meet someone and know within 20 seconds how he or she is as a person. If their energy is heavy I feel an awful pain and twist in my stomach. If they have good energy I feel light and airy.

We all have the ability to tap into this sixth sense, especially women. Although men can certainly tap into this power as effectively as women, it seems easier for us to do so. Take full advantage of this asset. You just need to quiet your mind and learn to tune into the right energy to feel it.

Everybody has this inner GPS system, but most people walk around with his or hers turned off. We have all said so many times, "I should have listened to my gut." That is your intuition and the Divine guiding you and telling you what to do. So listen to it. Learn to recognize the voice of your intuition and have the strength to heed its counsel.

Oftentimes, our intuition weakens when we are too afraid to follow its advice or it gives us answers other than what we'd hoped for. Ignore your intuition long enough, and it will a) weaken and/or b) find a way to get your attention in the form of a physical ailment, usually somewhere in your digestive system.

Intuition is like a muscle you must exercise—the more you practice listening to it and allowing it to guide the decisions you make, the stronger it will become. If you flex a weak muscle, you will struggle with the effort and not very much will happen. If that muscle is strong, however, you can physically feel it and command its power.

Intuition is no different. If you dig deep, listen to your intuition, and follow up with the courage it sometimes takes to stick to the path it lays out for you, you can never go wrong. You will move mountains.

## Practicing Intuition in Your Everyday Life

The third eye chakra—the one that sits right in between your two eyebrows on your forehead—is the source of all your intuition and guidance. This chakra is also known as the AJNA, which comes from the Sanskrit root that means, "to know, to follow, or obey." It is the monitoring center of your being and the chakra of your mind.

When you meditate with your eyes closed you look up and inward to this point. If it is open you will see a bright indigo color radiating in your mind. When this chakra is fully open it amplifies your creativity, imagination, and concentration, as well as your intuition.

You will see many Indian women cover this sixth sense area with a red dot or a jewel known as a Bindi. The Bindi is believed to protect the third eye, retain its energy, and strengthen concentration.

When faced with a choice, close your eyes and place your hand on your heart. As you weigh your options in making your decision, pay attention to how your body feels. Quiet your mind, and then breathe mindfully in and out through your nose at least five times.

Focus on your third eye chakra. Listen to your inner voice, and the answer to your question will reveal itself to you. The more you practice this technique the louder your intuition will speak to you, and you will learn to trust its voice every time.

**"As you become multisensory, you also become intuitive."**

- Gary Zukav

Smell, Taste, Touch, Sight, Sound and Intuition. When all these magically turn together, you are then connected to your higher and authentic self. Nourish your Soul with all of these daily. Try to align all of the senses as much as possible, this is how you really taste life and give essence to your spirit.

# A Woman's Health & Beauty

"A true woman's beauty comes from within. No amount of makeup or plastic surgery can create that quality of beauty, that inner light, that radiance."

- Yogi Bhajan

Your body is your temple and your vessel. It carries your spirit through your time here on Earth, so taking care of your health and vitality every day is extremely important. Like a beautiful ship sailing across the ocean, your body, your vessel, should shine as gloriously as your inner spirit does.

It is important to feel good about yourself. You should cleanse and bathe daily, take care of your hair, and live in the rhythm of your cycle. Everyone has a style that expresses their inner nature. Don't hide your true self in a costume; wear clothes that reflect your spirit and energy.

**"Elegance is when the inside is as beautiful as the outside."**

- Chanel

I have always loved fashion. I tend to wear lighter colors: beige, white, and bright bohemian colors are what resonate with my energy. I also try to wear as much cotton and silk as possible because they are soft and allow skin to breathe. I always wear my spiritual jewellery—my OM charms and Buddha's help me connect to my spirit. Your style could be very different, but wear whatever makes you shine from the inside out.

Most importantly, I am aware of everything I put into my body. I eat and drink healing and nourishing foods that take care of my body, skin, and nervous system. I have always been very conscious of what I eat, and I owe that to my mother, who raised us on everything from the health food shop.

She started giving us fish oil 35 years ago, and back then it was only available in a liquid cream form. Agh! Need I say more? Her efforts stuck with us, though, because all my brothers and sisters are really health-conscious eaters.

# *You Are What You Eat*

## *~ Beauty on the Inside ~*

Your relationship with food has a lot to do with how you operate in your day-to-day life. The 80/20 Rule applies to so many things, and food and drinking are no different. I love to have a glass of wine, and I drink several cups of espresso every day.

I love dessert now and then, and I especially love eating ice cream with my kids. On occasion, my husband and I will sit down on the couch at night after the kids go to bed with a tub of Hagen Daaz chocolate chip ice cream. I dig out the chocolate chips as he eats the vanilla ice cream.

I love entertaining, cooking, and going out to dinner. When I travel, I love to experience authentic local food, and I really appreciate culinary cuisine. It's truly an art form. I love a great vegetarian curry, Italian pasta, a real French Baguette with good French cheese, Pad Thai, and home made Middle Eastern food.

I just don't eat like this every day. I allow it into my life 20% of the time, and I never feel like I'm depriving myself of the pleasure of eating food and exploring different tastes, flavors, and experiences from all over the world.

I could write a whole other chapter on what I feed my kids, but it would be redundant. My children eat what my husband and I eat. We never catered to their whimsical tastes at a young age; we just fed them whatever we ate. They eventually figured out that if they did not eat what we gave them that they would go hungry.

My children drink veggie juice, and I have switched them to home made almond milk. This took a while, but I blended regular organic cow's milk with it and just kept diluting it until they could not tell the difference.

I rarely give my kids things that I would not eat myself. They eat more pasta, but I have switched them to gluten free pasta, as I eat a gluten free diet. It took me years to figure out that this was what was wrong with my digestive system. Gluten!

There are so many choices out there now—you can buy gluten free bread and pasta. Quinoa is gluten free, and it's an excellent substitute for rice. If you are going to give your kids rice, give them purple or brown rice instead of white. Give them multigrain bread, and cut out as much white as possible.

They eat a lot more sweets than I eat, though. They are kids, after all, and I don't want to deprive them of one of life's sweetest pleasures. It's just not all the time, and we don't keep sweets in the house. We buy them now and then, and we also take them out for ice cream. I am now starting to make them vegan, sugar free cookies and they love them.

Remember when your rewarding your kids with sweets that it should be in moderation. Don't make it a daily practice. It's better for their health and your sanity. If your kids are bouncing off the walls day and night, they could definitely do with less sugar in their diets.

If you put the effort and research in you will find so many recipes that are really healthy and also taste great. Health food has changed a lot over the years, not everything tastes like cardboard and hay like it used to.

What you put in your body and your children's bodies has everything to do with what comes out. You will feel more balanced, nourished, have more energy and less stressed when you are eating well. The same applies to your children. It may take some time to get yourself and your family onto a better daily eating plan, but that is ok.

Make subtle shifts to see more long-term dramatic changes. Don't look at it as a diet; adopt it as a lifestyle, and it will then just become part of your life. If you want to make the change you need to work hard at it and be religious for 40 days. Slowly change your family's eating plan, and once you have crossed that 40-day threshold it will become a lot easier to make it your lifestyle.

**"Every human being is the author of his own health or disease."**

- Buddha

## *Daily Eating Habits: My 80%*

Ayurveda teaches you that after the age of 36 we don't have the metabolism to take in more food than we can digest, so it is a lot better to eat smaller, more frequent meals throughout your day rather than three large meals.

Buy certified organic as much as you can and shop at your local farmers markets for the freshest and most healthy selections of fruits and vegetables. I love Whole Foods for their selection and quality. I know it is more expensive, but this is what you are putting in your body. It needs to be high quality. You wouldn't buy a Porsche and use the cheapest gasoline, so don't treat your body any differently!

I have priced out Whole Foods' 365-degree brand, and it is actually cheaper than most other products at other major grocery stores. Don't think that you can't get good food there at reasonable prices.

**"The food you eat can be either the safest and most powerful form of medicine or the slowest form of poison."**

- Ann Wigmore

## Morning

~ I try to start every day with a cup of warm or hot water with lemon in it (after my morning espresso). If you want something with a little more flavor, add a green tea bag in the water.

~ My breakfast every morning consists of an OM TONIC veggie juice, and sometimes, if I am a little hungrier, a slice of gluten-free wheat toast with avocado, sea salt, pepper, and lemon.

~ I love a soft-boiled egg sometimes, too, with a little sea salt and pepper.

~ A fruit or green smoothie is another great breakfast; add in any supplements you need here. I take omega 3 (fish oil caplets), a multi-vitamin, and a probiotic pill every morning.
* consult a doctor on your needs, everyone is different.

~ When I find my energy levels are low I drink organic liquid iron.

## Lunch and Dinner

~ I always eat either a homemade vegetable or lentil soup or a salad.

~ I love sushi. I eat a lot of fish and smoked salmon.

~ Quinoa is an amazing complex carbohydrate— lightweight, nutty, and relatively rich in protein for a grain.

~ I don't eat red meat. I have just started introducing organic free-range chicken into my diet for more protein, but that is on a rare occasion.

~ Sometimes I drink a smoothie or a veggie juice for a meal when I am not that hungry.

~ I try to eat heavier lunches and keep dinner light.

~ I try not to eat past 6pm, unless we are entertaining or out to dinner. Eating light helps you sleep more soundly at night because your body is not working that hard to digest food.

~ These are a lot of your super foods and greens that give you the substance and energy needed as a busy mother. I love and live on greens. Kale, spinach, and arugula.

~ Micro green salads are my favorite. I toss in sunflower seeds, tofu (the marinated one at Whole Foods has the most flavor) slivered almonds, tomatoes, cucumbers, avocado and finely chopped raw broccoli. To get more protein add some grilled organic chicken, smoked salmon or a cup of cooked Quinoa.

~ I always make my own dressing. 2-3 tablespoons of olive oil, a whole lemon squeezed, sea salt and pepper. You can also add a little fresh pesto in there and whisk.


### *Don't Forget*

~ Drink lots of water with lemon. This cleanses out your pipes and also keeps you full throughout the day so you won't eat as much.

~ Cut out soda and bottled juice. Replace it with sparkling water and squeeze fresh lemons and limes in there. (I love Kombucha from Whole Foods—this is a really good digestive for your stomach. The Gingerade is my favorite).

~ Cut sugar out as much as you can. If you want something sweet eat dark chocolate. Not only will it satisfy that sugar craving, but it's also good for you!

I recommend speaking to your health care provider about the supplements you need. The people at Whole Foods and in good health food stores can generally recommend you supplements if you are not sure of what you need.

Visiting a naturopath is also another option if you want more of a holistic point of view on what you need. My mom is a fantastic naturopath. She is just as knowledgeable as a doctor, so whenever I need something I consult her.

These are the foods that I eat, but only you can determine the appropriate diet for you. The suggestions are not intended to replace medical advice. Please consult a doctor before making any changes to your diet.

### Lifestyle Exercise

Exercise seems like a chore when you have not incorporated it into your life. When it becomes part of your life, you need it like air and water and it then magically becomes a major part of your lifestyle. Below is my typical weekly workout and meditation schedule.

1-2     90-minute Kundalini Yoga and meditation classes

1-2     60- minute Vinyasa Flow or JivaMukti Yoga Classes

1-2     60-minute Pilates Reformer classes

1-2     Power Walks (while the kids ride their bikes)

### Quick Exercise Sessions

I am a busy working mom and although I would like to always have a fixed schedule, my life just does not work like that. I have to be flexible and realistic about how much time I can dedicate to myself. So when I know I can't make it to a class, I do these following exercises at home regularly which get me through my day.

**5-15 Minute Meditation sessions** ~ listening to one of my many apps on my iPhone (information on these under my favourite OM things in the back of this book).

**3-7 Sun Salutations** ~ I get right on my Yoga mat at home in the middle of the day when I need to take a work break and just spend 10 minutes stretching and doing Yoga. I then sit for 5 minutes and meditate practising visualization.

**Mini Breath of Fire Breaks** ~ This is a powerful Kundalini breathing technique that brings you absolute peace and tranquility.

Sit comfortably in a meditation pose and close your eyes with your hands resting on your knees or in "Gyan Mudra". Close your eyes and mouth and breath rapidly in and out of your nose while pumping the belly in and out ~ do this anywhere from a minute to as long as you can push yourself.

If you want to balance your life, you have to incorporate exercise into your lifestyle. If you want to really rule your word, add Yoga and meditation to your formula. It will all change your life.

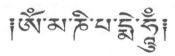

*Look at a diamond. Its brilliance and beauty emerges once it has been put under extreme pressure. When you have suffered, been in pain, struggled and experienced loss, you truly can then appreciate when life hands you something beautiful. You have a deeper appreciation of life and you radiate with beauty that has been created on the inside.*

**This is how beautiful people are made.**

*Inhale ~ Exhale*

## *Building a Spiritual Relationship*

You are a complete, whole person just as you are.

You don't need to meet someone to become ONE.

Instead, walk next to another, on your path through life, strengthen each other, and together you can take on the world.

I was not sure where to put this section on spiritual relationships, and at one point I was not going to even address it, as this topic could very easily fill a whole book. My intuition told me otherwise, and I wanted to at least address the topic of doing the work to build a strong relationship. After all, it is a major part of our lives, and when you start to do the work on yourself, you really will start to evaluate your relationships as well.

༄༅།ཨོཾ་མ་ཆི་པ་སྐྱེ་ཀྱོ།

A spiritual partnership is a relationship between two people for the purpose of spiritual growth. You commit yourselves to spiritual growth first as two separate individuals and then as a couple. To have a successful marriage or relationship, like anything else you want to be successful in, you first have to do the work on yourself. Once you become a whole individual, only then can you form a whole partnership with someone else. If you can't be an I then it is impossible to become a We.

When you work on yourself and start to become more spiritually alive, a shift will occur in your relationship. If your partner is willing to do the work with you, then you can grow and flourish together.

If you are the only one doing the work, however, you will encounter challenges in your relationship together. Sometimes the other person is not willing to change, or maybe they are not ready to do the work just yet. This is where the path that you walked together comes to a fork in the road. You must be prepared for this and willing to work at it.

The truth is that a great marriage or relationship will only stay strong for the long haul if you choose to grow together. The bond between spiritual relationships will still be rough, but you need these challenges that test your love, faith, and devotion in order to grow together.

I have been married now for almost 10 years. Like any couple, my husband and I have had our fair share of trials and tribulations. At times we adore one another, and at times we want nothing to do with each other.

One of my biggest problems was that I used to rely on my husband to make me happy. I thought that he could fill the voids in my life and within myself, and I expected him to make me feel whole. Wow, was I wrong.

I never grasped the concept that I had to work on myself and give those things to myself first. Now I don't feel empty because I know that everything I need, including love, is right here inside of me. When he gives, it's just icing on the cake.

I now know that my husband doesn't complete me—I am already complete. He just adds to the love and happiness I already have. If he was to stop giving that to me, I wouldn't feel empty because I have learned to give myself everything that I need to feel complete on my own.

I empowered myself when I learned to really love myself and feel happy about who I am on the inside. All of the insecurities and fear that I used to harbor just left me, and all I was left with was love, peace, and the feeling that I finally knew exactly who I was.

The biggest lesson I have learned though my spiritual growth is that when you get married or start a serious relationship, you don't become "One Person." This kind of thinking causes relationships to fall apart. This yearning to be as "one" and live within each other's spaces is very common in the honeymoon phase. In fact, it's completely necessary in order to form the kind of bond that sets you up for the long haul.

Once that powerful, euphoric feeling passes—once the high wears off—you both have to learn to be just you on your own. This is a normal part of any relationship, and it does not mean you have failed or have fallen out of love. This is the fork on your path to see if you both have what it takes to dig deeper and grow together on a more solid spiritual foundation. Romantic love does not last unless it has the ability to move and to evolve into something deeper.

This is an opportunity to really pass the test and see if your relationship has what it takes. Can you stay together on the same path for the purpose of spiritual growth? You have to be transparent to each other—completely open. How are you going to grow if you can't see the truth—the good and the not so good in each other?

You must become more aware of your Soul and operate in your partnership with a completely open heart. You must remove all of your armor and start to look at each other for who you really are. Let go of control and the need to always be right and let go of fear. Faith, patience, love, and prayer all come into play.

This is an opportunity to fall in love even deeper all over again and remember why you fell in love with each other in the first place. Two powerful and happy people walking side-by-side can take on the world together.

**"Love does not consist of gazing at each other, but in looking outward together in the same direction."**

- Antoine De Saint-Exupery

Remember that nobody can complete you in your life,

except for you.

# Relationship Mantra

If you want to improve your marriage or partnership, or if you want to meet a person to enhance your life, you have to be fully clear on what you want and know what you are looking for.

Take some time with your journal and write down a list of things you want out of your partnership, as well as what you want from the other person in your life.

Once you are done with your list, study it carefully and make sure it's what you really want.

Now that you have done that, put this heading on top of that list:

### *THE WORK I NEED TO DO TO ENRICH AND LOVE MYSELF.*

You see, once you can give all those beautiful gifts and love to yourself, you will never be lonely in love. You will never need to look outside of yourself again for affirmation of your worth.

This part of you is right inside and ready to shine. Learn to give it to yourself and your relationship will start to flourish and grow—that I promise you.

## I Am a Graceful Warrior Woman

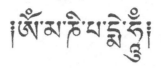

*{Prepared by Vanessa}*

**Whatever follows "I AM" in your words through life is what will come looking for you. Change your life by inviting this positive mantra into your world every day.**

I AM A SPIRITUAL GUIDE

I AM INSPIRATION

I AM THE MOST BEAUTIFUL REFLECTION IN MY MIRROR

I AM ALL I CAN BE AND MORE

I AM STRONG, I CAN BEND BUT I WILL NOT BREAK

I AM LOVE, THE DIVINE, THE SPIRITUAL AND INVINCIBLE

I AM A GRACEFUL WARRIOR WOMAN

Invite these words and energy into your life and watch the amazing things that will start following you. Do not waver. Do this every day for 40 days consistently and consciously, as often as possible throughout the day, and watch what happens. Little shifts will start, and then magic will appear in your life.

*Meditate on your Thoughts*

# The Nurturing Female Spirit

Everyone has a different role and story in life. Some mothers work full time, others part time, and many stay at home to devote 100% of their time to their families. Whatever role speaks to you the most is what you are meant to do.

Maybe your role does not involve being a mother at all. Whether you have not yet reached that chapter of your life, you are unable to have children, or you simply do not want kids, you still possess the nurturing female spirit. Some of you may be looking after ageing parents, animals, or in care of other people for your job.

Embrace this part of yourself as a woman, and do not be afraid to channel that nurturing energy toward whatever it is you care about. Whatever your role(s) now and in the future, devote yourself to them with loving care while devoting your love to yourself. You will blossom.

*Whatever you are doing, you must believe that you can have it all in life and feel fulfilled.*

*You just can't have it all at the same time.*

I have created a life in which I raise my children, take care of my family, and work for myself. I am blessed that I have had so many opportunities and have experienced so much by the age of 40. I now know what I really want in life; I now know love when it comes knocking on my door. If something does not resonate with me I gracefully walk down another path.

I feel like now is my time to do what I love while walking a slower path and raising my family. For the first time in a long time I am really taking care of myself—that's where the shift has occurred. I am a better person for my loved ones and in my career because I now make myself a priority.

I don't work 80 hours a week anymore. I balance my precious time between family, friends, travel, being creative, work, and looking after myself. That is basically the summary of the OM Formula; you just have to figure out what particular ingredients go into your mix. Find the things that allow you to operate as your optimal self.

By applying the principles of collective human wisdom and the ancient technologies for holistic well-being, you will feel fullness and richness beyond description. From this calm and happy place you will be able to handle your children, family, career, social life, and friends a lot more smoothly.

You will feel like the lotus flower that, even in the muddiest of waters and after the darkest of times, opens its petals to the light of the morning sun. With a holistic life of spiritual and bodily fulfilment, your true authentic self takes charge and leads the way.

Accept your day-to-day life as a true gift, look around you, and be grateful for all you have. Now is the time to stop living in fear and start living in the light of love. This is the place where you will control your life and your true destiny.

# Becoming a Mother

**"Of all the rights of women, the greatest is to be a mother."**

- Lin Yutang

## Falling Pregnant

While I was writing Om for the Mom a lot of women approached me about the struggle and pain of not being able to fall pregnant and start a family.

I have struggled on how to approach the subject because I cannot personally speak from experience, and I am not a specialist in this field. I was blessed to fall pregnant easily with my children, and for this I am eternally grateful.

So, I would like to share a story about a dear friend of mine that will capture your heart and, hopefully, light a candle in your world if you are struggling to fall pregnant right now.

༄༅།ཨོཾ་མ་ཎི་པ་དྨེ་ཧཱུྃ།

Tricia was 42 years old when she decided that she wanted to have a baby with her husband. After three miscarriages over the course of a single year, she was terribly concerned that she might never fall pregnant and become a mother.

A good friend of hers suggested fertility acupuncture. Tricia began a cycle of giving herself fertility shots and seeing the acupuncturist at the same time. She had regular ultrasounds to see if there were enough eggs, and during this time she tried to stay as optimistic and positive as possible. She also cut anything out of her life that caused her any undue stress or that may have blocked her energy.

She loved going to the acupuncturist, for her sessions they were both therapeutic and uplifting. In addition to performing acupuncture the therapist would also massage her back with an amethyst stone massage stick.

Spiritual healers say that amethyst heals physical ailments. It aids with the withdrawal symptoms of any sort of addiction, pain relief, pregnancy and preventing miscarriage, menopause, PMS, and general healing. Amethyst is associated with the brow and the crown chakras.

Tricia went on a trip over the Christmas holidays to visit her family, and she was at the airport when she felt that something was not right. She went to the bathroom and discovered that her period had come. She was devastated.

All those months of fertility shots and acupuncture, and now she was going to have to go through it again. Guilty thoughts crept in and ran through her head—I waited too long to fall pregnant. I am doing something wrong, etc.

She was not going to let these thoughts control her destiny. Her spirit remained strong, and she was determined to give it everything she had and not give in. She meditated as often as she could to visualize her newborn baby, keeping this reality within her realm of possibility.

She purchased an amethyst ring to wear, continuing with her acupuncture treatments and amethyst massages at the holistic fertility clinic. On the day before her next ultrasound visit, she was lying down in a state of deep meditation during one of her amethyst massages. In her mind's eye she saw a clear vision of a little spirit hiding behind something. She said, "Don't be afraid little one, come out from hiding. I will take care of you."

The very next morning, Tricia visited her doctor for another ultrasound. As the nurse probed her tummy with the cold wand, Tricia saw a strange expression on the woman's face. In a perplexed voice the nurse announced, "I am going to have to get the doctor to come in here to speak with you."

What was it now? She thought to herself. What possibly could be wrong with me now?

The doctor came in and sat down next to her. "Last week when we did the ultrasound there was nothing there, but something has happened," he explained. "This little thing was hiding and we didn't see it—we're so sorry for this oversight. You're pregnant. The baby has been there the whole time, and you're about four weeks pregnant. Congratulations."

Tricia immediately flashed back to her vivid vision from the day before. Her own words echoed in her mind. Don't be afraid little one, come out from hiding. I will take care of you. Stunned and elated at once, she sat down and just cried out of pure joy. A miracle had occurred in her life.

Today her happy and healthy little 7-year-old daughter, Sophia Belle, continues to be a shining, energetic, beautiful, and wise spirit. Sophia regularly tells her Mom that she chose Tricia to be her mother because she knew that she needed her in her life.

*Believe in the power of prayer, faith and miracles, and then anything and everything is possible in this life.*

### Pregnancy and Birth

I remember the feeling when I first found out that I was pregnant like it was yesterday. It was surreal, beautiful, and magical all at the same time. Words really can't describe it. Both of my pregnancies—with my daughter, Amira, and my son, Malek—were relatively easy. I was truly blessed to have fallen pregnant quickly, and apart from some back pain and the regular struggles you go though while pregnant, I cannot complain at all. For this I am forever grateful.

Throughout both pregnancies I ate well, indulged in Pre-Natal massages at least once a month, practiced as much Pre-natal Yoga as I could, and still continued to run around and work like a butterfly with a jet engine on. I remember having more energy during my last trimesters of both pregnancies than when I was not pregnant. I have heard similar experiences from a lot of women—I think God gives us an injection of energy to prepare us for the new life ahead.

The last few weeks were the hardest for me. I was on bed rest because my back could not support my huge belly, and I could not seem to find a position to lie in that gave me much relief.

When the time came to give birth, I had a few simple rules. Well one actually: get the epidural in as soon as possible! I think I reminded my doctor at least three times every visit.

I will never forget a conversation I had just a few short weeks after having my daughter. I was back at my spa and Yoga studio, and one of the Yoga teachers asked me, "Did you have a natural birth?"

"Yes I did," I replied. "It was great." I thought she was asking if I'd had a vaginal delivery rather than a C-Section.

"That's wonderful! I just don't understand how women take drugs to numb the pain and not feel the natural process of it all."

"Uh, no. I definitely had the drugs," I clarified. "The baby still came out the natural way."

How women choose to give birth is a personal choice, and it is a mother's right to do exactly what she feels is best for her. In Australia you can elect to have a C-section if you wish; you have a choice. Both of my children came out in what I call "the natural way," and both times I felt not an ounce of pain with my epidural.

The second time around my husband and I both agreed that he should not be in the delivery room. When he was in the delivery room the first time, during the birth of our daughter, he was hiding in the corner of the room, praying and breathing more heavily than I was. I think the doctors were ready to give him some kind of tranquilizer to just keep him quiet.

Some men are great about it all. It's wonderful if he wants to get in there with the video camera and be your cheerleader—go for it! But for those of you planning on having children or are pregnant already, if your husband or partner does not want to be in there, it's OK. It's really OK.

This does not mean they love you any less. It only means that they are just not built to see all of the "stuff" that goes on down there when you give birth. And there really is a whole lot going on down there, especially when you consider that the baby is not the only thing that comes out. Heck, even I did not want to see all that extra "stuff."

So women, if your partner feels more comfortable sitting outside then just let him be. Do not try to force him or guilt him into being by your side, or you might end up worrying if he's ok while you should be focused on giving birth!

Unless he tells you that there is absolutely no way in the world that he would miss it, you are probably better off letting him stand outside the door to peek in now and then and say hi. Trust me, you do not want anyone in that room who will cause you any undue stress while you're giving birth. You want that room calm and filled with the most Zen energy possible to make your experience as best as it can be.

I had aromatherapy oils burning and held onto crystals to calm my nerves, but ultimately it was my husband's nervous energy that had me clenching those crystals for dear life!

When my son was born, my sister was the only person allowed in the room with me aside from the midwife and doctor. She and I have a very synergistic connection, and we just get each other. She was so great.

She had pre-loaded a special birthing meditation playlist onto her iPhone, all ready for me to listen to with the earphones. She also spoke to me as if she were giving me a guided meditation the whole way through. I cannot recommend this highly enough to anyone giving birth—it calmed my nerves and opened up all my channels, making the whole birthing experience amazing. I was also fortunate that the midwife had a lovely, soothing energy, as well.

I was so relaxed that he came out in under 15 minutes, and the entire labor lasted less than 2 hours. The breathing techniques that I learned in meditation and Yoga really carried me through the whole birthing process. It was just a really beautiful experience.

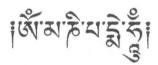

I am pretty sure that every woman in the world wonders how her life will change when she has children. This is a very natural and normal question to ask yourself, after all. Your life does change, but it changes for the better. The best, even.

There is no greater job, joy, or satisfaction in the world than being a mother because you are paid in pure love. It is one of the hardest jobs in the world, but the love you have for these beautiful little people you have created keeps you going.

My children have taught me how to better manage my life. I value the time I have with them, as well as when I am not with them. What I do and whom I spend time with have to mean a lot to me now. You figure out very quickly which people you don't have time for and who are really worth it.

Children teach you the real meaning of love, how to appreciate simplicity in life, and how to let go of things that are no longer important to you. I am a better person in every way because of them, both in my personal life and in my career. After taking care of my basic needs for happiness, they always come first—everything else is secondary now. But because I take care of myself and do all the work on myself, I have achieved a great balance in my life. I don't ever question what I gave up to have them and I'm happy to give them my all in life.

**"No one will ever know the strength of my love for you, after all... you are the only one who knows what my heart sounds like from the inside."**

- Kristen Proby

*A Pause on the Path:*

*Learning to Live the Slow Life*

**"If you determine your course with force or speed,
you miss the way of the law."**

- The Dhammapada Of Gautama The Buddha

I am writing in Turks and Caicos, a small island in the Caribbean. I came here with my family to relax, read, and write. The water here is magical. It is as turquoise as the brightest ocean you can imagine, and turquoise is my favorite color. The clearness reminds me of the most pure mind in meditation. Life here is so simple and peaceful; it is slow life in slow motion.

I felt I needed to really quiet my mind down and get away from day-to-day distractions to really focus on the inner voice inside. I have put away my computer and phone for a solid week and am quite happy to do so. While these two instruments are a big part of my life, they are also a big distraction from living the slow life. All I want to do is watch the ocean, walk in the sand, and be present. I want to play with my children, build sand castles, read, relax with my husband, and just be in the now.

When you are a busy family living in a big city, it is so important to make time for a retreat. It does not have to be an island getaway vacation; just take a drive to the country or someplace serene. Find some breathing space and spend time being present. This is an essential part of your formula and an OM pill that must be taken as often as possible.

You can't always be on vacation, and we all live in a world that is operated by day-to-day demands. To be in balance and find inner peace you have to learn how to stop and relax in your everyday life. Find a way to take a vacation within your own home and community.

I don't mean just sitting down to rest your body while letting your mind continue to run marathons. I mean you must shut everything down and quiet your mind to be able to enjoy the simple pleasures of life.

There are really only two ways to do this. One is sleep, and the other is meditation. If you are not getting at least seven hours of sleep every night you simply will not be able to function effectively in your day-to-day life.

I know that sleeping is a big problem for many people. At certain times in my life I, myself, have had such terrible insomnia that I have had to visit a doctor. I would invariably receive a prescription for a week's worth of sleeping pills to get my sleep back on track. After trying everything this was a last resort for me, and it worked. Once I regulated my sleep schedule I started sleeping on my own again.

Sleeping pills are really not the answer, though. They should only be used in extreme situations and only under a doctor's supervision. There are a lot of natural sleeping aids out there you can try, such as *Valerian, Melatonin, and a variety of sleeping teas. There are also quite a few smart phone apps that are excellent for helping you sleep and monitoring your sleep.

*These are only recommendations and do not replace a doctors opinion.

I love meditation. I can't talk about it enough, so I think you probably get that by now. As highlighted in the first section of this book, practicing meditation on a regular basis will change your life—I promise you. It will also help you sleep.

Meditation teaches you how to control your mind and quiet the racing thoughts that run though your mind every waking minute of your day. Many of us can't sleep because we stay awake "thinking."

*Did the kids do their homework? What will I make for their lunches tomorrow? What appointments do I have this week? Did I pay that bill? I forgot to answer that email. Did I turn the oven off?*

And the mind goes on. It never gives up its relentless work to occupy and control your life. It's like a nagging, annoying person just playing a tape over and over again in your head. Are you familiar with this voice inside your head?

Many of us are so used to it that we barely notice it, but it controls us, nonetheless. Meditation stops the tape to let you just be. Once you break the cycle—once the tapes stop playing in a loop in your head—you teach your brain how to sit in silence. Once you can command silence within yourself, sleep comes easily.

As a mother you need time to shut down. Take time away from your phone, TV, and computer—shut them down. Turn off the noise and get rid of the distractions. If you don't like what you hear in that silence, keep listening. When you present your true authentic self to yourself and bathe light on your shadow, you can then make the decisions necessary to change those things you don't like.

Your ultimate goal is to be in a constant state of joy at least 80% of the time—I think that's a realistic goal to live by. You can get there, but it does require a lot dedication and work. Nothing good in life comes too easily.

To experience that "high on life" feeling of joy, you must have gratitude. Thank your true self when you get there. Say, "I AM GRATEFUL" every moment that you can—this is an essential ingredient in your OM formula. "I AM GRATEFUL."

You must also learn to slow down. Stop and smell the roses. Look into people's eyes when you smile at them. Appreciate the little things that your partner, family, or friends do for you, and take joy in showing them small acts of love and kindness in return. Savor the quiet moments you have to yourself as sweetly as the sounds of your children's laughter.

*Patience and Peace*

**"Don't let the behavior of others destroy your own inner peace."**

- Dalai Lama XIV

It is said that a person who can master patience can master anything else in life. To live in the moment, breathe, and relax through challenging moments is probably one of the most difficult practices to master in everyday life. It is also the most rewarding, as it really is the ultimate vehicle to inner peace.

*Peace is not something to be found out there; the only place you find peace is in the stillness inside of you.*

It is easy to feel relaxed on a vacation and at peace while on a beach sipping a cocktail, getting a massage, or immersing ourselves in the luxuries of relaxation. The real challenge, however, is mastering inner peace and developing patience in day-to-day life. This is not so easy—not at first. This is where you have to do the work.

Once you can master your own inner peace, the next big challenge is not allowing others to destroy it. I consider myself to be a very calm, happy person most of the time, but the two people that push me to the limits are my children. I love them beyond words, but they can set off nerves and energy pathways in my body that I never knew existed.

Mothers, I know you can relate, and you are not alone in this department. When my children push me to the brink this "person" engulfed in flames arises inside of me at certain moments. My internal inferno blazes so powerfully that it takes every bit of my will power to calm my self-back down.

The one technique that has helped me tremendously to overcome these moments is a Kundalini meditation called "Breath of Fire." You have heard me talk about this method of Yoga a lot throughout this book, and I also dedicate a portion of the "Yoga" chapter to it; without a doubt, Kundalini has changed my life and helps me be a better mother.

Your children have picked you to be their mother, to teach them, to set an example, and to help them grow. Every day I try to remind myself that when I am in a challenging situation with them I have to teach them to know better. It may take 400 times to make the lesson stick, but that's my job. There is no greater test for developing patience and finding your inner peace than the lessons your children are teaching you every day.

Next time your 3-year-old starts a tantrum and throws his or her body onto the floor, you have two choices in the ways you can react:

- You can feed off their energy and perpetuate the negativity, learning nothing but what it feels like to hold onto anger.

- You can breathe through it and say to yourself "How can I stay calm and handle this without destroying my own inner peace?"

This is really important to remember. How you handle these situations is the very foundation of everything else you teach your children and, in turn, what your children teach you. Master this technique and I promise that your life will flow more smoothly, your family will be happier, and these testing times won't shake you to the core.

Take a deep breath. I firmly believe that your children have picked you to be their parent. Your children are right where they are supposed to be. You are right where you are supposed to be. You are working hard on becoming more mindful, on understanding normal developmental stages, on having realistic expectations, and on setting the tone in your home.

**"Never cut down a tree in the wintertime. Never make a negative decision in the low time. Never make your most important decisions when you are in your worst moods. Wait. Be patient. The storm will pass. The spring will come."**

- Robert. H. Schuller

## OM Mom Technique For Tantrums

Not a mother or parent on this planet has been spared the meltdowns and tantrums of our children. These moments test you to your core, and your lesson in these moments is Patience.

I started practicing the following technique six months ago. My husband laughs at me and still says, "They know you're a push over." But I think it works for me most of the time; at other times, I run to my room and lock the door (some would call that cowardly, I call it sanity).

When the confrontation and screaming starts, immediately walk over to them and stand over them tall and strong. Plant your feet firmly on the Earth, as you would in Tadasana (Mountain Pose) in Yoga.

Keep your hands open and firmly next to your body. Keep your head up high, chin up, and start breathing heavily in and out through your nose. Keep your eyes wide open and focused on them, using the Drishti practice of Yoga and meditation. This training technique helps you focus and overcome the challenge.

Stand there as long as you can. Do not move, do not waiver. Keep your shoulders back with your chest out and radiate strength. Do not lose it, keep yourself in control. Most of the time, after a few minutes, their screaming turns into laughter and they stop the behavior. At this time I take their hand, move them to a position where we are at eye level, tell them or ask them what they did wrong, and ask them to apologize.

## *Finding Breathing Space as A Mother*

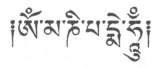

Sometimes you need to just need to step outside, get some air and remind yourself of who you are and who you want to be.

I meditate 15 minutes a day whenever possible. I get off phones, computers, and social media; I turn off all noise, sit in my meditation space, and go within. This recharges me, especially around midday. I meditate, practice conscious breathing, and then I have my lunch.

When I am really disconnected I drag myself to my meditation space and give myself 5 minutes. When my kids go to sleep, this is a great time for me to go into retreat, rather than getting on the phone or the Internet.

Sometimes, in the middle of my kids having a complete melt down, I run to my dark walk-in closet, put my iPod earphones in, and turn on a Deepak meditation. I breathe in and out very deeply, even if it's only for 5 minutes, and it leaves me feeling calm and centered enough to handle the situation.

If I can escape to my shower, I turn off the lights, light a candle, turn on music, and just let the water flow over my head. I sit on the floor and envision that I am at a retreat in Bali—I escape and find breathing space right in my own home, amidst the chaos.

Do this as often as you can. Create spaces within your own environment that surround you with serenity and solitude. Refer back to the first part of this book to design your personal sanctuary space in your home, and you can go on mini retreats every day.

### *Breathing Meditation Exercise*

### *To Calm Your Nerves*

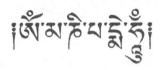

The first time I did this powerful breathing exercise in a Kundalini class, I literally decompressed and felt high on life. (This is when the idea for the front cover came to be of the Buddha holding the OM Pill).

You can be in the middle of any bad situation, with your kids throwing a tantrum, a co-worker confrontation or any moment where you are about to lose it. Step aside or turn away from the situation. If you can sit in a meditation pose, on the floor or on a chair do so, if you can't that's ok it will work just the same.

~ Close you eyes and focus on your third eye point (roll your eyes in and look up inside between the top of your nose)

~ Close your mouth and breathe in (like you're sipping air through your nose) 4 – 8 times through your nose very powerfully. The more you practice this the more breaths you can do.

~ Keep your eyes and mouth closed and release the air through your nose.

~ Repeat as many times as you can till you feel all the tension release.

# *Letting Go*

ZEN
禅

**"Children are natural Zen masters; their world is brand new each
and every moment."**

- John Bradshaw

I have always been a child at heart. I laugh a lot at my own jokes, and I believe that you have to laugh your way through any troubles life throws your way. If you don't laugh, you'll cry. You have to let it all out somehow, and there are so many ways to express and build positive energy.

Breathing, singing, listening to music, creating, dancing, running, walking, Yoga, riding a bike, skipping—just letting go in whatever way sets your spirit in flight. I sing in the shower all the time and put on pretend concerts for my kids.

Never lose that child-like state that's inside of all of us. As often as you can, get on the floor to roll around with your kids, jump on the bed with them, build forts and cubby houses, tickle them, and blow bubbles and raspberries on their little tummies. Play with them, for this time will soon pass, and one day you will miss all the opportunities you had to be a kid at heart with your children.

*Let go and let your spirit soar and you will start living, as you never have before.*

Raising children is one of the most rewarding but most challenging jobs in the world. It is not easy at all. I am a good mother, but I am far from a perfect one. Sometimes I just don't know what to do, and I don't know how to handle a situation. I've smacked my kids, I have screamed at them, and at times I have really lost it, to the point that if someone heard me they would probably commit me. On several occasions I have come this close to walking out of my own home and wandering the streets, just not knowing what to do.

Children will test you and push your buttons till you explode. You can feel peaceful and Zen one minute, and then—boom—that serenity is over. Sometimes I can mediate twice a day and go to Yoga and somehow, after all that, something they do will set me off.

My three-year-old son had a full-on tantrum in the store the other day, doing back bends and screaming like a wild banshee at the top of his lungs. I couldn't calm him down, so I just hid in the corner of the store praying for him to stop. You can't pull your Yoga mat out at that time and start doing downward dog can you?

To all the mothers out there reading this, let me tell you, you are not alone. It may appear to a lot of people that I have got it all figured out and that my life is balanced and perfectly Zen, but it's not. I will say this, though: if I did not continue to do all the work on myself, especially Kundalini meditation, I could possibly wind up playing a role in One Flew Over The Cuckoo's Nest. Any mother could.

Yoga and Kundalini meditation have saved and changed my life. As much as I would love to say I am a living, breathing Buddhist Monk, I am not. I am a human being—a female and a mother, at that—doing her very best to live a productive and positive life, make a difference in the world, and raise a family.

I often have a glass of red wine at 5:00 while preparing dinner just to calm my nerves at the end of a day. Sometimes that is all that gets me through my stressful times, especially if I did not get a chance to do Yoga that day. I drink alcohol in moderation, a glass or two a few times a week, and that's really it. I mainly drink red wine because it is loaded with resveratrol, an anti-aging ingredient found in the lining of the grape skin.

Most of all, though, what really gets me through it all is my kids themselves. I have always been a kid at heart, but they have taught me to open up and own that, without apologies. They keep me young, and it's the energy they bring me that helps me deal with the most trying moments. And even when I am completely unable to deal with those moments, I let it go and know that we can't get it exactly right all the time.

*The greatest challenge of adult life is to retain the wonderment of childhood even as you grow into your cloak of maturity.*

*Don't wear it as a burden, but let the light at the core of your inner being lift that weight.*

# *Leading By Example*

**"The way you talk to your children becomes their inner voice."**

- Peggy O'Mara

My three-year-old son looks so cute when he's doing Downward Dog (the Yoga pose). The first time I saw him do it, when he had just turned two, my heart melted. My little yogi does all sorts of poses—which he calls "doing yogurt"—and so does my daughter.

Although I had never actively encouraged or prompted them to do Yoga, initially, both of my kids seem like they may have been Yoga masters in previous lives. Where did they get it from? Me, of course. Since Yoga is such an integral part of my life, they have seen me practicing on enough occasions to want to do it, too.

Your children are absolute sponges when they are young, and they see and hear everything that you do and say. Everything. They are a million times more observant (and absorbent) than we are as adults, so it is important to remember what impressions they are getting from observing you.

You can guide them, teach them, talk to them, and coach them as much as you'd like (and you should), but those efforts will not add up unless your actions match your words.

Children begin to make powerful inferences about the world around them at a much earlier age than you might imagine. My son mirrors my Yoga moves and parrots the things my husband says or the things he hears in cartoons, but what else is he picking up?

Well, he takes cues from the way I speak to people and how I treat them. He hears the way I talk about life and my daily experiences, even when I don't realize that he's listening. In short, he is picking up everything.

I am not worried about the kind of example I am for my son and my daughter—I am confident and proud that I teach them well through both my words and my actions. I am far from perfect, and I make mistakes all the time; however, because I operate out of love and am comfortable with who I really am inside, I know that I am a guiding light to my children.

## *Teach Them Young*

My husband and I are trying to teach our children about living simply. I have always been blessed, and I realize that I have grown up with privileges that so many go without. I want our kids to be fully aware at all times that they should never take anything for granted, from the food on the table every day to the roof over their head.

Practicing simple but powerful exercises in gratitude and humility with your children will help shape them into grateful and giving human beings—two traits that are so important to develop in spiritual growth.

~ We limit the amounts of gifts they receive on birthdays and at Christmas; rather than buy them lots of toys we buy them books, put the money into our "Help the Homeless" jar, and add it to their education fund.

~ Quite often we go around the city and give money out to people on the streets in need. My 8 -year-old daughter finds a lot of joy in this act of giving.

~ We have taught out children to say thank you to God every time we put food in the fridge and sit down for a meal.

~ We monitor time on TV and iPads, which is a very difficult task to do these days, but it is so important to get your children involved in more creative and playful activities as much as possible.

~ We limit the time that we, ourselves, spend using electronic devices. This is important because children will take their cues from you. The less they see you on your phone or computer, the less they will want to use them.

# *OM Mom Tips*

## Yoga and Meditation for Your Kids

Now that my daughter is old enough, I have started taking her to Yoga and meditation classes designed specifically for kids. She, like my son, has been doing Yoga poses from a very young age, and she is finally ready to delve into Yoga as a practice. I am beyond happy that she has this opportunity at such a young age, and I know it will help her grow into a strong and centered young lady. I only wish that I had had the same opportunity when I was young.

Sit with your children as often as you can, on the ground with your legs crossed. Look at them in the eyes and ask them to breathe with you, closing your eyes and enjoying this life giving breath together. Teach them young that this simple and powerful technique can get them through any challenging moment in life.

"If every 8 year old in the world is taught meditation, we will eliminate violence from the world within one generation."

- Dalai Lama XIV

## 7 Daily Family Mantras

Empower your children while practicing and praying for patience to help guide these little Souls through this world. Consciously practice these seven mantras throughout the week and start saying them as often as you can. Frame this, put it on your fridge and invite them into your daily life.

- Our Family respects each other's individuality. We are all different individuals walking a path of unity and love. Let us all nurture each other along the way.

- Our Family embraces unconditional love. We give unconditionally, with love in the driver's seat. Love rules our world and our family.

- Our Family honors the truth. Let us live as honest, truthful human beings and always making truth our guiding light.

- Our Family lives in a constant state of gratitude. We are thankful for our daily blessings: food on the table, a roof over our head, and the health of each and every one of us. Everything God gives to us is a blessing, and we thank him every day for his kindness.

- Our Family yearns to Learn, Live and Grow. Lets live and explore the world together and learn as much as we can to help us grow.

- Our Family Pays It Forward. Every day we are consciously aware of how we can give back to others that need our support. Somewhere in the world, whether it is a family member or a complete stranger, a simple act of kindness can change someone's life.

- Our Family Prays. Daily we thank our Creator for the gift of life. We ask for help in remaining humble on our path through our journey together.

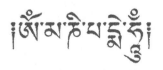

In Sutra 2, we have looked at how powerful a woman's strength can be and how you can master living in a permanent state of grace and gratitude. How you can work at building a spiritual relationship and a strong family. When you embrace your true Divine Feminine nature and couple that with Shambhala warrior strength, you can take on the world.

Have you ever looked at the nature of an elephant? These beautiful creatures are strong, gentle and kind. They walk their path in life, slowly and consciously, one foot in front of the other, with their feet planted firmly on the Earth. Little can knock them down. They are strong, but soft and powerful. They are beautiful and peaceful.

*This is how you need to walk your path in life. Embrace being a strong, graceful, peaceful warrior woman and you will be able to rule your life, your family, your career and your world.*

*It is then you can become anything and everything you want to be.*

# Bountiful AM I, Blissful AM I, Beautiful AM I MANTRA

**As women we are constantly nurturing others this mantra evokes calming moon energy for self-confidence and self-esteem so we can nurture ourselves.**

Sit comfortably, in a meditation pose, close your eyes, tune in, and chant this mantra for at least 11 minutes.

Bountiful Am I

Blissful Am I

Beautiful Am I

~ Prepared by Karampal Kaur ~

## *Grace of God Meditation*

**This mantra will channel your inner grace. It can turn your emotions into devotion and help you communicate effectively.**

**Part 1:**

Lie on your back, fully relaxing the face and body. Eyes are closed. Inhale deeply, hold the breath in, and silently repeat the mantra. **I Am The Grace of God** (10 times). Exhale all the air out, hold it out and repeat the mantra again (10 times).

Continue in this process of repeating the mantra 10 times on each inhale and 10 times on each exhale, for a total of 5 inhalations and 5 exhalations. A total of 100 silent repetitions.

**Part 2:**

Relax your breath, with eyes still closed very slowly come to sit up in Easy Pose (crossed legged)

Place the back of your right hand on your right knee in Gyan Mudra (index finger and thumb touching to form a circle holding the mudra gently but firmly) keep the elbow straight. Hold the left hand up by your shoulder with your palm flat and facing forward, as though taking an oath.

This time keep your breath relaxed. To help keep a count of your repititions, tense your left hand, one finger at a time, keeping the other fingers straight but relaxed. With each finger repeat the mantra out loud "I AM GRACE OF GOD" making a total of 5 repetitions out loud.

While repeating the affirmation, meditate on the governing energy of each finger.


Little Finger - MERCURY - power of effective communication

Ring Finger – SUN/VENUS - your vitality and physical health

Middle Finger – SATURN - your patience and calmness

Index Finger – JUPITER - your wisdom

Thumb – Represents you and the positive ego.


"Grace of God meditation will give you self-effectiveness. It is designed that way. Any woman who does it will find grace in her behavior. It may take a little time, but the results will be positive."

*Yogi Bhajan*


~ Prepared by Karampal Kaur ~

# I AM A DIVINE FEMININE MANTRA

*{By Vanessa}*

*Sit quietly at the beginning and at the end of everyday and chant this I AM Mantra to connect to your divine feminine nurturing spirit.*

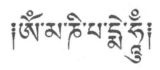

I AM PURE FEMININE SPIRIT

I AM A LOVING MOTHER

I AM AS PERFECT AS GOD INTENDED ME TO BE

I AM A CHILD AT HEART

I AM PATIENCE

I AM PEACE

I AM LOVE

I AM BEAUTIFUL ~ INSIDE & OUT

I AM A JEWEL IN THE LOTUS FLOWER

# SUTRA 3

## *Dreams and Passion*

**"It is never too late to be what you might have been."**


- George Eliot

One of my greatest blessings is that I have always been able to develop creative outlets through my work and experiment with so many different kinds of career experiences by the age of 40.

My passion for creating is a big part of who I am. It's as vital to me as air—I would not be able to live and breathe without it. I have built businesses, created global brands, and developed revolutionary products, but my greatest accomplishment was creating my two beautiful children. The love you have for your children burns brighter than any candle and becoming a mother is a gift and a life commitment. Nothing else will bring you greater joy.

My second greatest accomplishment is that I have created a life that I am proud to say is my own—a life that I want to live. I have a loving, supportive husband and family who are my biggest fans. They push me whenever I doubt myself. I have a wonderful group of friends that I consider my family, and I am blessed to have many great friends all over the world.

What I know for sure:

> *Keep company of people who are going to*
> *inspire and lift you higher.*

I am walking on the path that God intended for me. I know this because I feel it in every cell, every heart beat, and in the warmth of my Soul. A fortune-teller, a spiritual guide, and my energy healer all told me several years ago that I would be teaching empowerment, spirituality, Yoga, and conscious holistic living to other women. I did not need their assurance because I already knew it inside. I believed it and that's all that you need.

> *The best way for you to predict your future is*      *for*
> *you to create it.*

I am eternally grateful for my place in this world. I feel complete. It took me a lot of work to get here, but I am at peace inside. The wholeness inside of me at times could leap out of my heart. I am grateful for my determination and stamina, and I am blessed to have discovered all the ancient technologies that help me chart my course through these modern waters. I am grateful for all of my lessons and all of the trials and tribulations. I am grateful for my family. I know that love conquers all things.

I thank God for guiding me to get out of my own way to let the sun shine on my beautiful life. I trust that I will be given everything I need to keep walking the path I have found in this life.

I hope that my experiences and words can serve as a glimmer of potential in your mirror. I hope you see the possibilities that life has in store for you. You just have to believe and do the work on yourself.

Once you start doing the work on yourself, subtle shifts will occur. Sometimes bigger aha moments will happen, but change is a slow process. It is really the small differences and the decisions you make in your daily life that will lead you down your path.

Do whatever you do in life with integrity, honesty, and love. Don't worry about the money. It will flow. Keep moving on your path, and the Universe will inspire you. If you light your candle, God will light a thousand more along your path. Do everything in your life with intention, and have the courage to be who you want to be. Love and respect yourself, and everything will fall into place.

You don't need healing or fixing by a guru. You are your own guru, your own strength, and your own power. You are a magnificent, beautiful being and the master of your own destiny. You already have all the answers and all of the miracles that you will ever need inside of you, waiting to emerge from your Soul. You just have to do the work to find them. Believe in this power within you, and you will change your life.

We are all lotus flowers emerging from the muddy waters of life, and every day we have the chance to wake up and open our petals to the light of the morning sun. If the sun is not shining, look for the rainbow at the end of the storm. We are all lotus flowers floating in a vast, glistening ocean of existence and opening each and every day to the same source that gives us life.

The little OM pill of life is waiting for you to take—your own personal formula for a life full of love, peace, happiness, and abundance. Endless refills and fully abundant. Just remember that it will only work from the inside out. You and you alone hold the key to the kingdom of your dreams and the beautiful, fulfilling life that you are meant to live. The Universe is waiting for you to create your formula.

Now is the time to get out of your own way, awaken your spirit, move those mountains, and let the sun shine down upon you.

"So I say to you. Ask and it will be given to you; search, and you will find; knock, and the door will be opened for you."


- Jesus of Nazareth

*~ Namaste ~*

*Look for the dream that keeps coming back.*
*It is your destiny.*

Everyone on this Earth has a path and a purpose. If you have a life and you are still breathing then you have a purpose. God needs you to be in service of others with your talents. To find this path you have to learn to become fully present in your day-to-day life.

***Find your authentic self, ground yourself as a graceful, warrior woman and then go build your dream career or business.***

There is something inside of you that you can do better than anyone else in the world. This is how the Divine made you. Your work is to find your passion embrace it, and let it shine. With your unique talents, you can offer the world the power and love that can help elevate our Universe.

Once you do the work things will become clearer, and the inner voice at your core will speak louder. Embrace serendipity and realize that you are walking a journey that is constantly unfolding before you.

When you are doing what you love in life and following your bliss you will know it. Time will pass quickly and you will immerse yourself in what you are doing effortlessly.

***Do what you love and you will never work another day***
***in your life again.***

When all of your thoughts, attitudes, and intentions begin with "I AM" and "I CAN," followed by whatever it is you want out of life, the Universal Source will transform your life to align with the words of the song that your Soul wants to sing. The Soul is infinite, and all it wants to do is expand. The way to expand it is by doing the things you love.

To be the change you want to see in the world you don't have to be loud. You don't have to be extremely intelligent or the best looking person. You just have to do the work, be committed, and show up. When you see that God has created a space for you in this Universe that only you can fill—a place for you to illuminate your passions and serve others—that is when you will stop "looking for yourself."

*SOAR TO GREAT HEIGHTS, AND THE WINDS WILL CARRY YOU TO FLY.*

*BELIEVE BIG AND PRAY BOLDLY. ALLOW THE DIVINE TO FLOW THROUGH YOU, AND YOU WILL EXPERIENCE THE GREATEST MAGIC AND BLISS IN YOUR LIFE.*

My love for visual storytelling and creative expression has always been embedded in my Soul. It is who I am, and I cannot breathe without it. As far back as 2nd grade, I remember always decorating my math and writing homework with flowers and love hearts before handing it back to the teacher.

I was so lucky to know who I was in that essence at an early age; however, as a creative type with an entrepreneurial vein running through me, I run into the problem of wanting to do everything. There is no end to what I visualise in my mind's eye, but also I have a powerful yearning to take that vision out into the world and shine the brightest light on it possible. I am a Gemini in my Eastern Sign and a Rat in my Western Sign, a combination described by famed astrologer Suzanne White as, "A butterfly with a jet engine on it." That's me. Funnily enough, my name Vanessa means butterfly.

The day I turned 15 I wanted to go get a job in the local bakery. I remember seeing the sign in the window and thinking to myself,

"Wow, how great to actually work to earn your own money and feel empowered." I proposed the idea to my family at the dinner table one night and they said, "You don't need to work right now." I remember saying, "But I want to work." That has never changed for me, and I have been eternally blessed throughout my life to be able to always find my passions in life and then go out and build my dreams.

After finishing school at the Chicago Art Institute at the age of 22, I wanted to start my own business. I thought that I could never make it as an artist, and "starving artist" did not sound like an appealing job title to me. So, I became a fashion designer. After 10 years in that business, I realized that "starving fashion designer" should probably be an equally well-known cliché because it is very hard to make money in that profession. I loved creating that's all I knew.

I was 22 and knew nothing about business, so the road ahead of me was going to be rough.

My first fashion collection made it into Nordstrom's. The famous stylist Patricia Fields was buying my collection for her very hip New York boutique (before her years as a stylist for Sex and the City), and my shirt design made it onto the front cover of YM (Young Miss) magazine.

One problem: I wasn't making any money. I could sell ice to Eskimo's, create, design and market, but I couldn't make money.

One day my father said words to me I will never forget. "Everyone does fashion, yes they all do it differently, but you're all competing for the same slice of pie. Do something really different. Invent something no one else has done and build on that."

His words sat with me for some time. I was creating new designs every day in my collections, always getting inspired by a piece of fabric. I was creating things that others were not doing. But that is not what he meant. He meant:

**Get outside the box, and if you want to really get noticed, remove that box completely.**

With this new insight at the age of 24, I invented Hippies, the world's first Low Rise Hipster Hosiery and underwear brand. It was 1997 and the worldwide fashion industry was bombarded by low-rise fashion. The high-waisted clothing of the 80's had passed, but nobody in the intimate apparel industry was addressing the underwear problem. I was either cutting the tops off of mine or rolling them down to accommodate all of my new low-rise fashions.

The light bulb went off one day while I was in my closet getting dressed to go out. So, Hippies was born—"pantyhose and underwear for the Hip." With a small team we took the brand globally in a little over a year. Within 18 months we were in over 1700 stores around the world, including Nordstrom's, Macys, and Bloomingdale's in the US markets.

Patricia Fields and many other fashion boutiques around the country picked up the brand. We had a list of celebrities sporting their Hippies a mile long, and the brand even made it onto the OPRAH show alongside Victoria Secret on one of her shows on how to wear things better.

I travelled the world overseeing manufacturing and designing, holding press events, and selling. For the next 7 years I became a butterfly with a jet engine on my back—I didn't stop. But eventually I got tired and burnt out.

All the big major global brands started copying us, and the business of being creative was turning into a business of developing commodity products. 80% of our sales were 20% of our product line: black opaque tights and white, black, and nude hipster underwear. I no longer had room to be creative, and I felt it was my time to stop. I slowly wound down, and we finally got an offer from another company to sell. By the end of it all though I walked away with not one penny.

It took me a long time to really understand what footprint I left from all my efforts, blood sweat and tears over those 7 years. One day, only about a year ago did the light bulb go off for me.

*"I steered a revolutionary design into the billion dollar plus a year intimate apparel market and shifted a stagnant market with one simple idea. To this day my simple invention is now seen on millions of women around the world."*

Leaving the fashion business was bittersweet. As much as I loved it, there was more about it that I did not love. I knew I was making the right decision to journey a new path. Those 7 years in that business taught me so much about building a company and a brand. Those lessons were invaluable. I was almost 30, though, and I felt like I was in the middle of a "one-third-age-life crisis." I had no idea what to do next.

It was then I magically fell onto a Yoga mat. This was when I really started embracing Yoga and spirituality, and I realized I could live large in a very small space – who knew? That's when the shift in my life started happening, where I knew I could thread this powerful tool of spirit into my business and life.

I wanted to be a spiritual entrepreneur and spread this light to others.

There is a whole new market and breed of spiritual entrepreneurs and holistic consumers out there that is growing and gaining more momentum and market share every day. They care about the world, sustainability, philanthropy, the environment and they are paying it forward. They take care of themselves and care about what they put inside their bodies. They are not defined by their age; they are defined by their spirit. They are creative, they consult their Soul and their boardroom is right inside of them ~ they go within themselves all the time for answers.

They are a power to be reckoned with ~ mentally, creatively, physically, and spiritually. They are Generation OM.

- Don't be scared. Go out there. If you fail, at least you tried doing something you love. Everything is a lesson in your degree of life, and you will learn something from everything you do. True failure is sitting there never attempting anything in life.

- When others are going left, go right.

- Do something you love. Everyone has a talent that's been given to him or her; they were born with it. Find it and contribute in service to others. The money will follow.

- If you're not in your dream job, create your dream business on the side from home. Make products and sell them on Etsy or EBay. Make it happen!

- The Internet makes anything possible. You can build a website, offering your products or services in America today and start trading with someone on the other side of the world tomorrow.

- Create a formula for your life that gives you little tastings of your joy. You will build and attract more of it when you put the intention out there.

- Have the power to see the future, the wisdom to learn from the past and the discipline to live in the moment.

# *Bhakti Mantra*

*Tunes into the frequency of the Divine Mother Power. Practice it to overcome your fears and insecurities and fulfill your desires.*

## Complete Mantra:

Adi Shakti, Adi Shakti, Adi Shakti, Namo Namo
Sarab Shakti, Sarab Shakti, Sarab Shakti, Namo Namo
Pritham Bhagvati, Pritham Bhagvati, Pritham Bhagvati, Namo Namo
Kundalini Mata Shakti, Mata Shakti, Namo Namo

## *Translation:*

I bow to (or call on) the primal power.
I bow to (or call on) the all encompassing power and energy.
I bow to (or call on) that through which the divine creates.
I bow to (or call on) the creative power of the Kundalini, the Divine Mother Power

"Merge in the Maha Shakti. This is enough to take away your misfortune. This will carve out of you a woman. Woman needs her own Shakti, not anybody else will do it. When a woman chants the Kundalini Bhakti mantra, God clears the way. This is not a religion, it is a reality. Woman is not born to suffer and woman needs her own power."- Yogi Bhajan

{Prepared by Karampal Kaur}

# My Favorite OM Things

## *Yoga and Meditation Music*

Most of these are available on I TUNES or www.spiritvoyage.com

**Deva Premal** ~ Into Silence

**Jai Jagdeesh** ~ The Expansive Spirit

**David Newman** ~ Leap Of Grace ~ The Hanuman Chalisa

**Master Choa Kok Sui** ~ OM The Sound of Stillness ~ 108 Om's

**Snatum Kaur** ~ Grace

**Sat Kartar** ~ I Am, I Am

**MC Yogi** ~ Elephant Power

**Yoga Flow Mix 1 Jala** ~ Desert Dwellers

**Shantala** ~ The Love Window

**Sacred Circle** ~ Amrit Kirtan

## *MEDITATION APPS*

~ Hemi – Sync Relaxation and Sleeping App (I TUNES)

~ Deepak and Oprah Meditations

Visit Deepak's website for a wide range of great of meditations you can purchase.

www.deepakchopra.com

Visit www.spiritvoyage.com for a wide selection on meditation and Kundalini Apps and Music.

*BIRTHING MEDITATION ALBUM*

Birthing Through Hypnosis ~ Kristin and Eliot Nemzer (2010)

*MINERAL BATHS* -Ancient Minerals Magnesium Chloride bath salts. Place a cup into a hot bath and add a few drops of your favourite oils. Mine favourite aromatherapy blend is Ylang, Ylang and Sandalwood. These minerals will penetrate to cellular level and relax you.

*YOGA* - Visit www.yogajournal.com to find a Yoga studio near you. There is a wealth of information on this site about anything in the Yoga world as well as healthy holistic living.

Kundalini Yoga - www.3ho.org and www.KRI.org

Sat Nam Yoga Chicago – www.satnamyogachicago.com

Jivamukti Yoga – www.jivamuktiyoga.com

Samgha Yoga  Chicago– www.samghayoga.com

Exhale Spa (National) – www.exhalespa.com

Kripalu – www.kripalu.org

*PRANIC HEALING*

www.pranichealing.com

*HOLISTIC FOOD*

www.healthyfoodrawdiet.com

## *DONATE TO GREAT CAUSES*

www.friendsoftheorphans.org

www.amanikids.org

www.lifestraw.com


## Connect to our Tribe


Stay connected to everything OM FOR THE MOM, all my favourite things, recipes, Yoga and Meditation, music, experiences, quotes and tips. From our site you can connect to Instagram and Pinterest, where all the pretty visuals live.


www.omforthemom.com

www.facebook.com/omforthemom

www.twitter.com/vanessaspalmer


Connect to our blog and sign up on the mailing list on our website for weekly updates and tips. Don't worry, we have a Zen approach when it comes to marketing and we will not bombard you with too much information ~ just the right amount of love.

## BOOK TOUR AND OM PHILOSOPHY WORKSHOPS

We will be planning several book tours and workshops around the world so stay connected to find out where we will be. If you want to recommend an OM FOR THE MOM workshop/retreat and book signing in your local Yoga, meditation or holistic space, please reach out and we will move mountains to make it happen.

## OM PHILOSOPHY RETREAT

We are now planning the 2014 OM PHILOSOPHY retreat. The location is still to be decided; we are planning either the Caribbean or Mexico at a magical sanctuary. This will be a 5-day, escape to a beautiful destination that will change your life and nourish your Soul.

I will be designing and leading the woman's retreat that will be made up of ~ Yoga, meditation, women's empowerment sessions, creative career workshops, holistic food preparation, Ayurveda, beauty and wellness and relaxation.

A week of pure bliss. Stay connected to us to find out more information and how to sign up to join our tribe and walk your journey of a lifetime.

**Sign up on our mailing list at~**

www.omforthemom.com

## My Favorite Spiritual Library of Books and Inspirational Resources

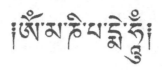

**I AM WOMAN** ~ Yogi Bhajan

**A COURSE IN MIRACLES** by Helen Shucman, Foundation For Inner Peace

**PROOF OF HEAVEN** by Eben Alexander, M. D.

**EAT, PRAY, LOVE** by Elizabeth Gilbert

**SHAMBHALA**: The Sacred Path of the Warrior by Chogyam Trungpa

**RULING YOUR WORLD**: Ancient Strategies For Modern Life by Sakyong Mipham

**THE TIPPING POINT** by Malcom Gladwell

**THE SEVEN SPIRITUAL LAWS OF YOGA** by Deepak Chopra, M.D. & David Simon, M.D

**BUDDHA**: A Story of Enlightenment ~ Deepak Chopra

**THE SEVEN SPIRITUAL LAWS OF SUCCESS**: A Practical Guide to the Fulfilment of Your Dreams ~ Deepak Chopra

**THE SHAMBHALA PRINCIPLE**: Discovering Humanity's Hidden Treasure ~Sakyong Mipham

**THE VALKYRIES** by Paulo Coelho

**THE ALCHEMIST** by Paulo Coelho

**CONVERSATIONS WITH GOD**: An Uncommon Dialogue, Vol. 1 by Neale Donald Walsch

**THE POWER OF NOW**: A Guide to Spiritual Enlightenment by Eckhart Tolle

**A NEW EARTH:** Awakening to Your Life's Purpose by Eckhart Tolle

**THE BHAGAVAD GITA**~ Anonymous

**THE CELESTINE PROPHECY** by James Redfield

**TUESDAYS WITH MORRIE** by Mitch Albom

**THE FIVE PEOPLE YOU MEET IN HEAVEN** by Mitch Albom

**THE SECRET** by Rhonda Byrne

**90 MINUTES IN HEAVEN**: A True Story of Death & Life by Don Piper, Cecil Murphey

**THE DALAI LAMA'S BOOK OF WISDOM** by The Dalai Lama XIV

**THE ART OF HAPPINESS** by The Dalai Lama XIV, Howard C. Cutler

**THE UNIVERSE IN A SINGLE ATOM:** The Convergence of Science and Spirituality by The Dalai Lama XIV

**THE FOUR AGREEMENTS:** A Practical Guide to Personal Freedom by Miguel Ruiz

**THE TIBETAN BOOK OF LIVING AND DYING** by Sogyal Rinpoche, Andrew Harvey

## *Glossary of Terms and Eastern Philosophies*

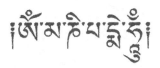

**Asana** ~ A Yoga movement, position, pose or posture, and the names of almost all Yoga poses end in "asana"

**Aum** ~ The universal mantra, cosmic vibration of the Universe, represents the four states of consciousness, Sanskrit word meaning "all"

**Aura** ~ In parapsychology and many forms of spiritual practice, an aura is a field of subtle, luminous radiation surrounding a person or object

**Ashtanga Vinyasa Yoga** ~A style of Yoga found and popularized by K. Pattabhi Jois, and which is often promoted as a modern-day form of classical Indian Yoga

**Balasana** ~ Yoga Position, Child's Pose

**Bikram** ~ is a system of Yoga that Bikram Choudhury synthesized from traditional hatha Yoga techniques and popularized beginning in the early 1970s. All Bikram Yoga classes run for 90 minutes and consist of the same series of 26 postures and 2 breathing exercises. Bikram Yoga is ideally practiced in a room heated to 105°F (≈ 40.6°C) with a humidity of 40%

**Chakra** ~ Literally meaning "wheels", in Yoga this refers to the seven energy or "life force" centers lying from the base of the spine to the head

**Chanting** (e.g., mantra, sacred text, the name of God/Spirit, etc.) is a commonly used spiritual practice. Like prayer, chant may be a component of either personal or group practice. Diverse spiritual traditions consider chant a route to spiritual development.

**Chi~** In traditional Chinese culture, is an active principle forming part of any living thing. Qi is frequently translated as "life energy", "life force", or "energy flow". Qi is the central underlying principle in traditional Chinese medicine and martial arts. The literal translation of "qi" is "breath", "air", or "gas"

**Complete Breath** ~ Breath exercise of even inhalation and exhalation that involves all respiratory muscles

**Drishti** ~ or focused gaze, is a means for developing concentrated intention. It relates to the fifth limb of Yoga (pratyahara) concerning sense withdrawal, as well as the sixth limb dharana relating to concentration

**Guru** ~ Spiritually enlightened Soul, who can dispel darkness, ignorance and illusion from the mind and enlighten the consciousness of a devotee/disciple, Teacher, spiritual preceptor, spiritual teacher

**Gong Bath** The gong bath is an immersion in sacred and healing sound wherein the gong master activates the full sonic potential of the gong and bathes the listener with sustained waves of primordial sound. During a gong bath, listeners typically experience a sense of connectedness and peace as the sacred sound of the gong clears blockages and restores the free flow of vital energy throughout the body. Some Yoga and Meditation studios incorporate the gong bath into classes

**Hatha** ~ also called hatha vidya, is a system of Yoga described by Yogi Swatmarama, a Hindu sage of 15th century India, and compiler of the Hatha Yoga Pradipika

**Jivamukti Yoga** ~ As a path to enlightenment through compassion for all beings, Jivamukti Yoga is grounded in the original meaning of the Sanskrit word asana as "seat, connection" - relationship to the Earth

**Karma Action** ~ The act of doing

**Kriya** ~ Activity, dynamic yogic practice

**Kundalini Shakti** ~ Refers to the human's potential energy lying dormant in muladhara (base) chakra like a coiled serpent. When awakened it rises up through the sushmuna nadi

**Kundalini Yoga** ~ Philosophy expounding the awakening of potential energy and inherent consciousness within the human body and mind.

**Lakshmi** ~ Goddess of prosperity and beauty; consort of Vishnu

**Maha Bandha** ~The great Kundalini lock - combines the three locks in Yoga - the moola bandha, jalandhara bandha and uddiyana bandha - together with breath retention

**Malasana** ~ Garland Pose

**Mantra** ~ Sound of syllables repeated by Yogis to produce a change in consciousness

**Mantra Pramatribhava** ~ State of meditation in which the breath becomes balled and enters the central channel for the rise of Kundalini

**Mantra** ~ Subtle sound vibration, which through repetition aims at expanding one's awareness or consciousness

**Meditation** ~ A state of complete silence and inner awareness, reflection, a process of introspect

**Mudra** ~ Literally means 'gesture' - mudra expresses and channelizes cosmic energy within the mind and body

**Namaste** ~ is a common spoken valediction or salutation originating from the Hindus and Buddhists in the Indian Subcontinent and also in Japan. It is a customary greeting when individuals meet, and a valediction upon their parting. A non-contact form of salutation is traditionally preferred in India and Nepal; Namaste is the most common form of such a salutation

When spoken to another person, it is commonly accompanied by a slight bow made with hands pressed together, palms touching and fingers pointed upwards, in front of the chest. This gesture, called

Añjali Mudrā or Pranamasana, can also be performed wordlessly and carries the same meaning

**Nirvana** ~ is an ancient Sanskrit term used in Indian religions to describe the profound peace of mind that is acquired with moksha (liberation). In shramanic thought, it is the state of being free from suffering. In Hindu philosophy, it is union with the Brahman (Supreme Being)

**OM** ~ The universal mantra; cosmic vibration of the Universe; represents the four states of consciousness (also Aum)

**Om Mani Padma Hum**~ Mani means "jewel" or "bead" and Padma means "the lotus flower", the Buddhist Sacred Flower

**Padmasana** ~ Lotus pose - a seated meditative posture, "lotus posture", sitting position in which each foot rests on opposite thigh

**Para vedha** ~ An experience of the rise of Kundalini where one feels a flow of sexual joy

**Prakasha** ~ Inner light

**Prana**~ Vital energy force sustaining life and creation, Breath, life, vitality

**Pranayama** ~ Technique of breathing and breath control, which regulates energy, flow and aims at maintaining energy balance

**Raja Yoga** ~ Yoga in which union is achieved through concentration of mind

**Sadhak** ~ Spiritual aspirant or student

**Sadhana** ~ Quest, spiritual practice

**Salamba Sirsasana** ~ Headstand Yoga Pose, Supported Headstand

**Salambhasana, Shalabasana** ~ Locust Yoga Pose

**Samadhi** ~ Final stage of Yoga in which concentration becomes one with the object of concentration; supreme union, absorption, state of God consciousness, realization of one's own nature, the eighth of the eight stages of classic Yoga

**Samsara** ~ The process of a worldly life, the cycle of life caused by birth, death and rebirth

**Sanskrit** ` A language used in of Yoga, Hinduism and Buddhism, and an official languages of India, considered "historical"

**Sara Swati** ~ Goddess who bestows knowledge of fine arts and power of speech

**Sat Nam** ~ Truth. Identity

**Satsang**~ A session of devotional singing, chanting or meditation

**Savasana** ~ Yoga Corpse Pose, sava "corpse" asana "pose"

**Shakta Vedha** ~An experience of the rise of Kundalini in which Kundalini takes the form of energy.

**Shakti** ~ Vital force, energy, power, mediator between individual and universal, the force of manifestation in the Universe, often depicted as female

**Shambhavi Mudra** ~ A Yoga gesture in which one focuses at the mid-eyebrow center

**Sukhasana** ~ A comfortable meditative Yoga pose; also called the 'Yoga easy pose' or simply the cross-legged pose

**Sūtra** ~Is an aphorism (or line, rule, formula) or a collection of such aphorisms in the form of a manual or, more broadly, a text in Hinduism or Buddhism. Literally it means a thread or line that holds things together

**Tadasana** ~ Mountain pose, palm tree pose, used in many forms of Yoga

**Upanishads** ~ A collection of Hindu spiritual writings following from the Vedas

**Vedas** ~ Four ancient texts- Rig, Yajur, Sama, Atharva, which are further divided into Samhita, Brahmana, Aranayaka and Upanishads. They were revealed to the sages and saints of India which explain and regulate every aspect of life from supreme reality to worldly affairs. The oldest books in the library of mankind

**Yoga** ~ State of union between two opposites - body and mind; individual and universal consciousness; a process of uniting the opposing forces in the body and mind in order to achieve supreme awareness and enlightenment, from the Sanskrit Yoga meaning "to join together or yoke"; a system of techniques to enable the joining of the physical and emotional/spiritual bodies

**Yoga Sutras** ~ A collection of concise aphorisms on the aims and practices of Yoga as collected and written by the scholar Patanjali

**Yogi** ~ One who has attained Yoga, or union of the two bodies, one who practices Yoga on a committed basis.

# Sarah Lyn Palmer

{Editor}

Sarah Palmer is a writer and editor. She has a B.A. in Human Development Psychology and currently lives in Chicago. Lately, when she's not busy with social media marketing and writing web content, she enjoys photography, Yoga, meditation, song writing, time spent with good people, and being out in nature as much as possible.

# Karampal Kaur

{Contributing Writer on Kundalini}

I first met Vanessa when she laid her mat down in one of my evening Yoga classes. A few after-class discussions later, it was evident that our paths had crossed for a reason. Besides being a devoted yogini and a loving mother, Vanessa's down to Earth approach and her desire to connect with others about her life's direction falls in line with what many spiritual beings and life coaches possess: a calling to share. I'm grateful and honored to be a part of such an invaluable resource for women. This book is truly accessible and contains crucial information for our fellow Shakti's on how to embrace their sacredness and grace to truly live as the vibrant women we were born to be.

As I sat down to write and tell you more about me, I connected the dots of my experiences and it was clear that they added up to be much more than special moments in time. They were each steps on a journey that led me to Kundalini Yoga, and ultimately to my whole self. In essence, my story begins and ends in the same place—within myself—though I didn't know this for a long time.

Those who know me know I am a typical Sagittarian—I just can't sit still! I was born with an adventurous spirit, then caught the travel bug in my early 20s and have traveled the world since. At the risk of sounding cliché, I was Soul searching. My curiosity put wind in my sails and my quest began. Being in nature for a few months out of the year was my reset button from the hustle of my busy city life in Chicago. Along the way, I was fortunate enough to form meaningful relationships that I believe have molded me into who I am today. My eyes have been blessed by Godly scenery, I have meditated in temples, sat in Satsangs (spiritual lectures), swam in every lake and ocean I could find, hiked up volcanoes and mountains, visited anyone who would open their doors, meeting my fellow humans and appreciating them for all that they were. But even with all of these spiritual riches, I found myself still searching.

By my early 30s, I had what most people hope to attain. I had two successful businesses—a thriving career as a hairdresser and co-owner of Beauty Mark Salon and founder of Ireations Jewelry—as well as a few investments abroad, a little money in the bank, and my wonderfully supportive family. I seemed to have everything, so why didn't I feel fulfilled? I thought perhaps I was just too picky. I kept telling myself that I just needed to enjoy what I had, but I still felt that undeniable emptiness in the pit of my belly. Then the unexpected happened. A few months shy of my 33rd birthday, I met my partner and I also found what I was searching for: me.

My love affair with Kundalini Yoga began in 2006, when my partner opened my eyes to the teachings of our beloved Yogi Bhajan. I had practiced Yoga before, but nothing compared to this. As I chanted my first mantra, my body was buzzing. I remember being a little nervous—pushing out these ancient sounds past the frog in my throat was tough, but I knew I was safe, so I decided to throw myself into the experience. My eyes began to well up with tears; I didn't know what was happening to me! I began to feel euphoric and was excited for what else would happen. Thirty-one minutes had passed and the recording of the mantra I was chanting with slowly faded away. The world was so quiet and steady. The tears continued to flow and were definitely joyful now. I felt the weight of the world lift as my oneness with all that exists began to sink in. I even felt compelled to giggle at God's sense of humor, who was watching over me, wondering when I would realize that I had been searching for what already lived inside of me. I am happy to say that my search ended that day. I was empowered by the truth, the missing piece, and the Divine light. Many people talk about out of body experiences, but this was an *in body* experience. I had traveled across the world, but only that day had I returned home to myself.

That day, Kundalini Yoga made me whole, and today, my greatest joy comes from teaching it. My passion for sharing its benefits with others stems from my own life experience of its power to create ease and flow in life.

To help me fulfill my life's purpose, I've been blessed to study with the most knowledgeable teachers at the Kundalini Research Institute in New Mexico, and to continue my training to teach prenatal Yoga with renowned yogini Gurmukh. I've organized events to benefit local and international charities and sit on the board of directors at I Grow Chicago NFP, facilitating Yoga training and activities for at-risk youth in the Englewood neighborhood.

In November 2010, my partner Siri Adi and I opened the doors of Sat Nam Yoga Chicago, a Kundalini Yoga and Wellness Center that offers a platform for teachers and students to bloom. Creating a spiritual, holistic community is my calling, an experience of trust, truth and overall physical, emotional and mental wellness. I teach every chance I get throughout the week and host monthly New Moon and Full Moon Group Meditations, Healing Circles, and a Sacred Circle Women's Kundalini Yoga and Lifestyle Class (that I hope you find your way to someday). My mission is to present these practices in a safe, effective way to help anyone who is ready for change.

Blessed are women and mothers who have the strength to manage busy lives and families and find the courage to still hold true to who they are. Together as beautiful women, let's continue to find, know, replenish, support, and celebrate each other and ourselves every day. The first step is to go deep within, as the answers and the truth are already inside.

**Sat Nam** (*truth-identify*)

With love of the divine and blessings for all that you hope to become,
*Karampal Kaur*

For classes and more information on the transformational practice of Kundalini Yoga, visit www.satnamyogachicago.com

Mention OM FOR THE MOM and your first class is on us (new students only)


To find a teacher near you, visit 3HO.org and KRI.org. Special thanks to the Kundalini Research Institute for permission to publicize the teachings of Kundalini Yoga as taught by Yogi Bhajan® .

*Dream at night, that anything in life is possible.*

*Dream at night that your wings emerge for you to take flight.*

*Dream at night in colors you never knew existed.*

*It's time to come out of your cocoon and fly, little butterfly.*

**Namaste.**


*It is time for you to take your journey. Your jewel has emerged
from the Lotus Flower.*

Made in the USA
Lexington, KY
15 September 2015